Carbon Shinai
カーボンシナイ

- CF-Type
- DB-Type
- K1-Type
- K2-Type

Orange   Red   Yellow

The official Carbon Shinai rubber stopper have been improved.

The NEW official rubber stopper
¥300 (Domestic price in Japan)

WARNING!!
Never use anything other than our official rubber stopper on your Carbon Shinai !!

When in use of your Carbon Shinai.....

1. To prevent injury, be sure to use our official rubber stopper. Do not use stoppers made for conventional bamboo shinai on your Carbon Shinai, as there is a risk of injury to your opponents if the tip distorts or the piece of shinai slips out from the rubber stopper and penetrates through their men-gane. (men grill)

2. When choosing a saki-gawa (tip leather), make sure that it is more than 5cm in length and completely covers the official rubber stopper. If the saki-gawa is shorter than 5cm, there is a risk of injury to your opponents if the piece of shinai slips out and penetrates their men-gane.

3. Whatever the reason, do not shave the surface or cut the length of your Carbon Shinai. If you shave or cut, the Carbon Shinai will get damaged to result in injury to your opponents.

4. Always check the condition of the surface of your Carbon Shinai before, during and after use. As soon as you notice any damage, stop use of the shinai immediately. There is a danger of injury to your opponents if your Carbon Shinai gets split or broken.

5. When tying the naka-yui (leather binding), either tie a knot in the tsuru-ito (cord), or tie one end of the naka-yui to the tsuru-ito, or by another means ensuring that it does not move up and down during use. If there is any damage whatsoever to the saki-gawa, tsuka-gawa (hilt), rubber stopper, tsuru-ito and so on, replace them immediately with new ones.

6. If the tip of the Carbon Shinai get damaged, or a slat is protruding out of the saki-gawa, there is a danger that it could penetrate your opponent's men-gane and injure them.

Kendogu Revolution

Mu-Jun Men
武楯面

WARNING!!

1. Under no circumstances should organic solvents (such as thinner, alcohol, benzene, toluene, acetone, gasoline, kerosene, etc.), acidic or alkali chemicals, domestic cleansers, car cleansers, or anti-mist sprays, be used to clean the shield. These substances will cause the shield to deteriorate, leading to clouding, cracking or breaking, thereby resulting in danger of injury to the face.

2. Should the shield develop deep scratches or cracks on either the outer or inner surface, discontinue use of the shield immediately, and replace it with an undamaged shield. If the shield is used in such a condition, there is a danger of its breaking, causing injury to the face.

3. It should be fully understood that, as with the traditional Japanese Kendo-Men (mask), there is still the danger of injury to the face through fragments of broken bamboo or Carbon Shinai pieces penetrating through areas not covered by the shield.

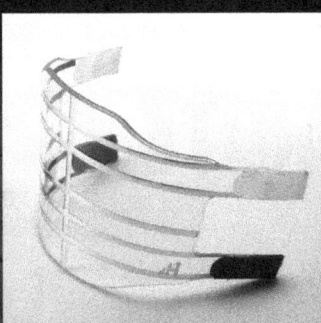

SG-Type

- SCIENCE TO SEEK SAFETY -

HASEGAWA
HASEGAWA CORPORATION

WEB : http://kendo.hasegawakagaku.co.jp/
Email : contact@hasegawakagaku.co.jp

Carbon Shinai — Points to be checked

DANGER !! — Before these happen..... — **ATTENTION !!**

Although the Carbon Shinai is much more durable than conventional bamboo ones, it will inevitably be broken since it is a Kendo sword which is beaten hard and thrust over and over again. Inspect the condition of the surface, sides or reverse of the Shinai's pieces before, during and after use, and stop use of the Carbon Shinai immediately should the damage like the following pictures be observed. (The pictures are just one examples of many.)

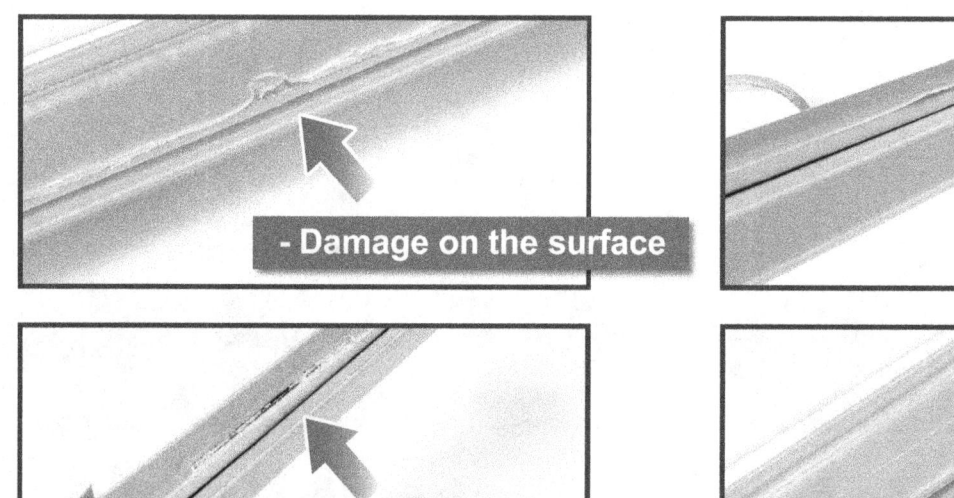

- Damage on the surface
- An unglued surface sheet
- Exposure of the Carbon fiber
- Longitudinal crack on the surface
- Damage and ungluing of the surface
- Crack on the reverse

There is a case that the reverse gets cracked even without any damage on the surface. Inspect the inside of the Shinai by pushing pieces with fingers unbinding the Naka-yui.

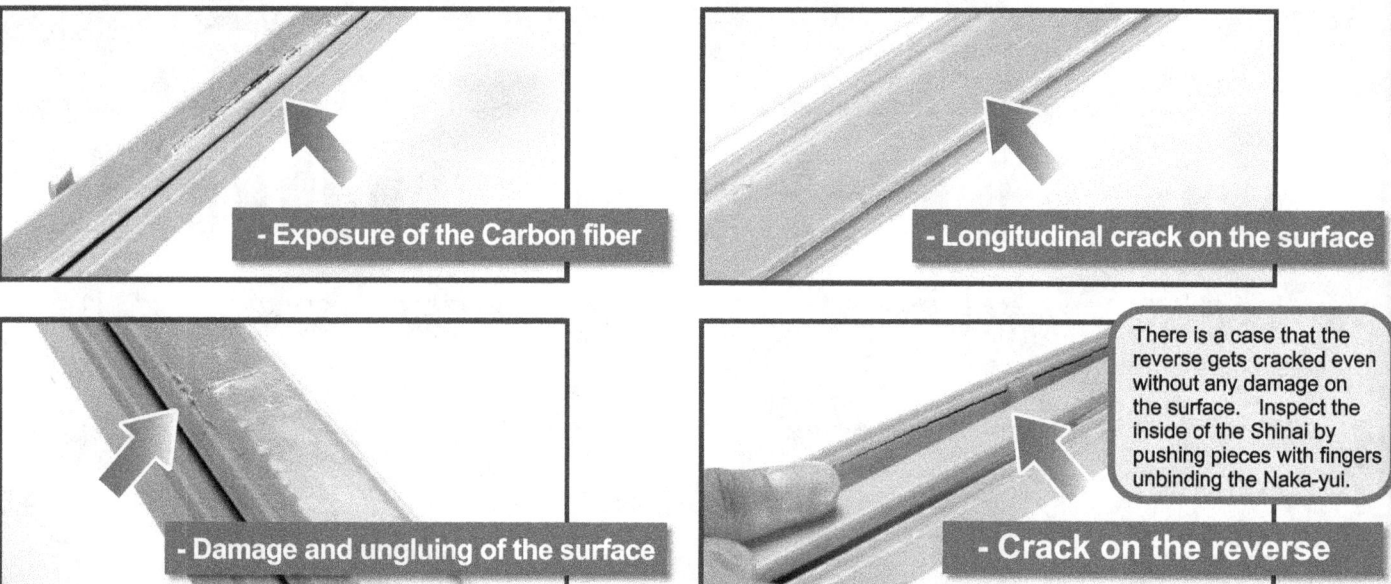

HASEGAWA-KOTE

- Detachable and washable "Tenouchi" is easy to wash and dry.

- "Tenouchi" is replaceable when it torn. No need to repair.

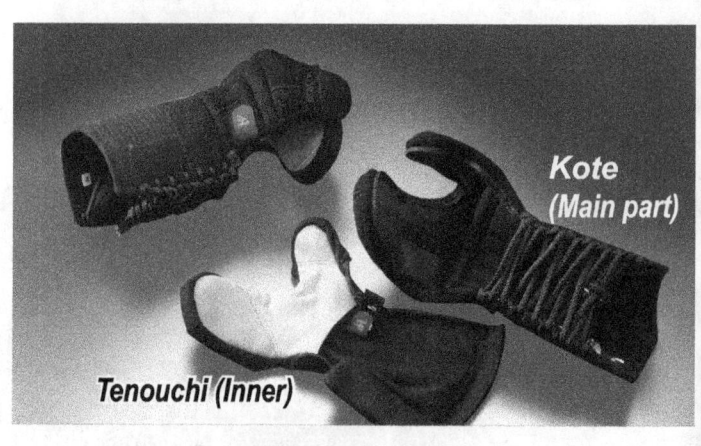

Kote (Main part)

Tenouchi (Inner)

- SCIENCE TO SEEK SAFETY -
HASEGAWA

HASEGAWA CORPORATION
http://kendo.hasegawakagaku.co.jp/

... Custom Made with Delicacy and Pride

IN JAPAN.

www.chibabudogu.com

ADVERTISEMENT

剣 禅 書
KEN ZEN SHO

THE ZEN CALLIGRAPHY AND PAINTING OF YAMAOKA TESSHŪ

Yamaoka Tesshū (1836-1888) was a Japanese master of the sword, Zen and calligraphy. This full-color book on the Zen art of Yamaoka Tesshū features reproductions of extremely valuable calligraphy pieces, and also a number of essays about the relationship between swordsmanship, the study of Zen, and calligraphy. All of the works presented are translated into English, and its significance explained in detailed captions. Some fantastic specimens of Zen calligraphy by Tesshū's famous contemporaries Katsu Kaishū and Takahashi Deishū (Tesshū's brother-in-law), and modern master Terayama Tanchū are also featured.

Yamaoka Tesshū (1836–1888)
Dragon (cursive script) 1885.
Sumi ink on paper 130cm × 56cm.

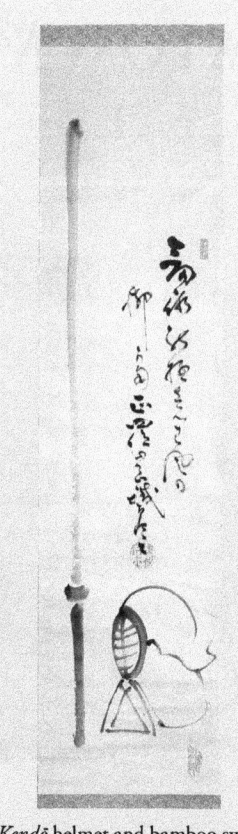

Kendō helmet and bamboo sword
(with inscription in cursive script) 1886.
Sumi ink on paper 130cm × 30cm.

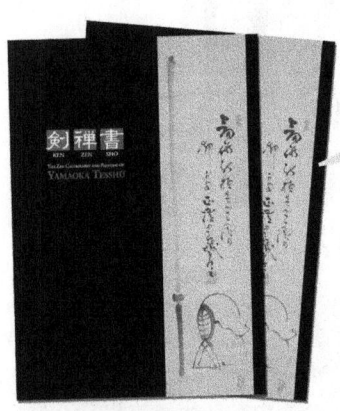

Size:A4 Colour/Black&White
ONLINE STORE PRICE IS
US $ 64.95
+ SHIPPING & HANDLING

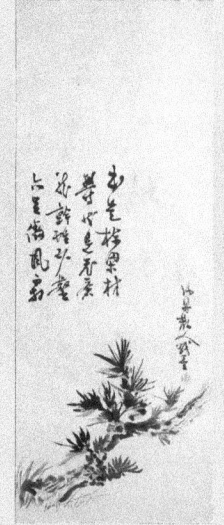

Katsu Kaishū (1823-1899)
Pine (with inscription in cursive script) 1895. *Sumi* ink on paper 134cm × 53cm.

Takahashi Deishū (1835–1903)
One line saying (cursive script) 1900. *Sumi* ink on paper 134cm × 64cm.

Terayama Tanchū (1938–2007)
One line saying (cursive script) Autumn 2004. *Sumi* ink on paper 164cm × 33cm.

To order, visit **www.kendo-world.com** more information, mail to **info@kendo-world.com**

Published by BUNKASHA INTERNATIONAL CORPORATION / Suga 488-1-501, Onjuku, Chiba, Japan 299-5106

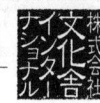

KENDO WORLD Volume 6.4 June 2013 Contents

Editorial _____ 2	On Being Captain _____ 42
Kiwada Daiki Interview _____ 4	Kendo That Cultivates People Part 14 _____ 46
Hanshi Says Aoki Hikoto (Hanshi 8-dan) _____ 7	Living with Shikai: Generalized Anxiety Disorder in Kendo _____ 52
sWords of Wisdom "Remember, then forget" _____ 10	Getting to Grips with Who You Are _____ 56
The Nuts 'n' Bolts of Kendo Effective Training Methods—Kirikaeshi _____ 12	A Cognitive Neuroscience Perspective on 'Enzan-no-Metsuke' _____ 58
Reidan-jichi Part 15 Kihon Dōsa Part 4 _____ 13	Red Sea Kendo—Kendo in Israel _____ 60
Unlocking Japan: Part 24 Gaijin Style _____ 17	The Spirit of the Samurai Lives on in Montreal: The Collection of Dr. Richard Béliveau _____ 61
The 43rd Kanagawa-ken Yonsha Taikō Kendo Taikai _____ 18	Naginata Tournament Simulation: A Method for Training Tournament Staff _____ 67
The Kendo Coach: Sports Psychology in Kendo Part 9: Aggression in Kendo No. 4 _____ 20	Shinai Sagas Duelling Ground _____ 72
The Budapest Sakura Cup in Hungary _____ 25	In a Galaxy, (Not That) Far, Far Away... Kendo and Women in Turkey _____ 75
A Comparative Analysis of Bushido and Chivalry _____ 26	Women's Kendo in Chile _____ 78
My Adventures Practising Kendo and Iaido _____ 31	The Naginata Dantai Taiteki no Kata _____ 80
It's Not Gods Who Bake the Pots —The Journey of the Russian Kendo Team to the 2013 European Kendo Championships _____ 34	Bujutsu Jargon Part 4 _____ 88
	Martial Aids _____ 90
A Swordsman's Evolution: Comparing Miyamoto Musashi's *Heidōkyō* to Later Writings _____ 39	Book Mark Kendo—A Comprehensive Guide to Japanese Swordsmanship" _____ 91

Kendo World Staff
- Bunkasha International President & Editor-in-Chief— Alex Bennett
- Bunkasha International Vice President & Graphic Design— Shishikura 'Kan' Masashi
- Bunkasha International Director— Michael Komoto
- Bunkasha International Director— Hamish Robison
- Bunkasha International Director— Michael Ishimatsu-Prime
- Bunkasha International General Manager— Baptiste Tavernier
- Senior Consultant— Yonemoto Masayuki

KW Staff Writers / Translators / Photographers / Graphic Designer / Sub-editors
- Axel Pilgrim PhD
- Baptiste Tavernier MA
- Blake Bennett MA
- Bruce Flanagan MA
- Bryan Peterson
- Charlie Kondek
- Gabriel Weitzner
- Honda Sōtarō PhD
- Imafuji Masahiro MBA
- Jeff Broderick
- Kate Sylvester MA
- Lockie Jackson PhD
- Miho Maki
- Paul Benson
- Scott Huegel (MaSC)
- Sergio Boffa PhD
- Stephen Nagy PhD
- Steven Harwood MA
- Stuart Gibson
- Taylor Winter
- Tony Cundy
- Trevor Jones
- Tyler Rothmar
- Vivian Yung

KW would like to thank the following people and organisations for their valuable cooperation:
- All Japan Kendo Federation
- Chiba Budo-gu
- Hasegawa Teiichi - President, Hasegawa
- *Kendo Jidai* Magazine
- *Kendo Nihon* Magazine
- Nippon Budokan Foundation
- TOZANDO

Guest Writers
- Aoki Hikoto (Kendo Hanshi 8-dan)
- Balázs Czifrik (Hungarian Kendo Federation)
- Chris Cocks (Canadian iaidoka living in Shizuoka)
- David Groff (Meiji University)
- Evgeny Andreev (Russian Team Manager)
- Francesca Baradit (Kai Ken, Vina del Mar, Chile)
- Kurt Schmucker (US Naginata Federation, Vice President)
- Ido Slonimsky (Israel National Team)
- Jon Fitzgerald (GB Team Captain)
- Merve Giray (Turkish Kendo Federation)
- Nakano Yasoji (Now deceased. Kendo Hanshi 9-dan)
- Ōya Minoru (Prof. International Budo University; Kendo Kyōshi 7-dan)
- Ryan McIntyre (Victoria University, Wellington)
- Sakae Eri (Osaka University of Health and Sports Science)
- Sumi Masatake (Kendo Hanshi 8-dan)
- Taylor Winter, Michael Wrigley, and Darryl Tong (Otago University)
- Thomas Sluyter (Renshinjuku Dojo, Amsterdam, Holland)

COPYRIGHT 2013 Bunkasha International Corporation. No part of this publication may be reproduced in any form whatsoever without written permission from the publisher, except by writers who are permitted to quote brief passages for the purpose of review or reference. Kindly contact Bunkasha International Corporation at info@kendo-world.com.

Editorial Conventions Used in KW Inevitably in a magazine of this nature, many non-English words appear in the text. Japanese words are italicised and include macrons (ū, ō) etc., apart from common place names and nouns, and words in some captions and headings. As a general exception, KW treats all the martial arts (budo), such as kendo, iaido, jodo, ranks, and so on as Anglicised words without using macrons. Japanese names are written in accordance to the traditional Japanese manner of family name followed by given name. Traditional *ryūha* are written with capitals and therefore are not italicised. 'Kata' with a capital 'K' refers to the set of Nippon Kendo Kata, and *kata* refers to set forms in general. The masculine personal pronoun is used throughout the text in some articles in the interest of readability, and is in no way meant to slight the significant contributions made by female kendoka.

Editorial

By Michael Ishimatsu-Prime

Alex has once again delegated responsibly for the editorial to me. *Konkai mo yoroshiku onegai shimasu.*

Every year from May 2-5, kendoka and budoka descend upon Kyoto, the former Japanese imperial capital, to watch or take part in the Kyoto Embu Taikai each year. It is held at the Butokuden, the Hall of Martial Virtue, near the Heian Shrine. This year's event was the 109th. There are demonstrations of iaido, jodo, naginata and kobudo, and kendoka graded R6-dan and above are able take part. There are also many different *keiko-kai* that take place in the Kyoto Budo Centre located behind the Butokuden, as well as at other venues around the city.

The Kyoto Embu Taikai is not a competition in which victors progress to the next round. Rather, each match is a 90-second bout where the fighters demonstrate their skills and technique in front of Japan's top sensei, and hundreds of onlookers. This was my first visit for a number of years, and I had forgotten what a special event it was. I was surprised to see just how many people I knew and had trained with that were there, both Japanese and foreign.

Perhaps the most inspiring event was the sight of the last two Hanshi 7-dan kendoka starting the Hanshi section (meaning that they received higher billing than the K8-dan sensei) on the final day. Ōta Hirokata-sensei from Osaka was 99 years old, and his younger opponent, Makino Noboru-sensei from Aichi Prefecture, was a sprightly 90. "*Shōgai kendō*" is an oft-mentioned phrase that means "lifetime kendo", and this was proof of what is possible in kendo. I hope that I am still around at their age, never mind practising kendo.

Another highlight of the Kyoto Embu Taikai was the bout between H8-dan Sakudō Masao-sensei from Osaka University of Health and Sports Science, and H8-dan Hamasaki Mitsuru-sensei of Tokyo. This was an enthralling encounter, although not one strike was even made: a battle of *seme* versus *kamae*. Hamasaki-sensei, winner of the All Japan 8-dan Competition in 2009, is known for his strong *kamae* and *seme*, and repeatedly he pressured Sakudō-sensei who held firm. Sakudō-sensei was also unable to break down Hamasaki-sensei's *kamae* and create an opening. It appeared that the crowd also had a lot invested in this fight. When the *shimpan* signalled the end of the match, you could feel the tension lifting throughout the Butokuden as the onlookers broke into applause.

The fight between Hamasaki-sensei and Sakudō-sensei was the epitome of *katte-utsu* – win first, and then strike. Neither could win first, and so neither could strike. It demonstrated just how far I have to go in kendo. As was demonstrated by Ōta-sensei and Makino-sensei though, if I look after myself, I still a little while to get there.

At the Kyoto Embu Taikai this year, of the 3554 participants, 12 were foreigners. The increase in the number of foreign spectators and participants led to them being featured in a segment on "Sports Japan", a program on NHK World. R6-dan Donatella Castelli from Italy was interviewed along with her opponent, as was KW's own Alex Bennett. The Kyoto Embu Taikai is an example of the Kendo World motto "*kōken mukyō*" —"Crossing Swords and Borders". Participants of the 1st Kendo World Tokyo Keiko-kai held at the Nippon Budokan on June 30, 2012, received a commemorative *tenugui* with this written on it. Incidentally, the 2nd Kendo World Tokyo Keiko-kai will be held on Saturday July 20, 2013, at Meiji University and we are looking forward to seeing you there.

Following on from the 2nd Kendo World Tokyo Keiko-kai, the next big date in the international kendo calendar, apart from the Foreign Kendo Leader's Summer Camp in Kitamoto, is the 2nd Sport Accord World Combat Games which will be held in St. Petersburg, Russia, from October 18-26, 2013. Aside from kendo, these games include events for aikido, boxing, judo, jujitsu, karate, kickboxing, Muay Thai, sambo, sumo, taekwondo, wrestling, and wushu. This year's event has been expanded to also include savate and fencing. Of these, five are already Olympic sports, although wrestling will be controversially removed from 2020.

There will no doubt be discussion, not from the AJKF, however, on whether or not kendo should be made an Olympic sport. Personally, I never really took this matter seriously before. If anything, I thought that as long as kendo could retain its integrity, it would be beneficial to expose it to a wider audience. However, at the 25th International Seminar of Budo Culture (March 8-11, 2013) there was a lecture titled "The Internationalisation of Karatedo". It made me realise that an unchanged Olympic kendo would not be possible. In his lecture, Kurihara Shigeo-sensei (Vice-President of the All Japan Karatedo Federation) detailed the difficulties involved in getting karate recognised as an Olympic sport, and the changes that were being made out of necessity to meet the Olympic criteria. A video that was produced to promote karate's case for inclusion in the Olympics was shown, but received considerable ridicule from the attendees, both karate practitioners and others. An instructor from a Japanese university karate club commented to me how truly sad it was.

Karate is much more mainstream than kendo, especially overseas. If karate has to go through what seems like compromise after compromise to gain Olympic status, what changes would kendo have to make? Would there be video judging, as is being trialed in Korea (see KW 6.1)? Would competitors have to wear different coloured *gi* and *hakama*, as judoka do? Perhaps the Combat Games is a much better forum for the promotion of kendo worldwide, and as this event grows in size and stature, it will be to the benefit of kendo without necessitating concessions. (By the way, karate's bid for inclusion in the next Olympic Games was unsuccessful.)

Tokyo is a candidate city for the 2020 Olympic Games, and if its bid is successful, kendo may well be included as a demonstration event, as it was in 1964. However, as Japan's politicians seem to be doing their utmost to sabotage their chances of hosting the Olympics with nationalistic, sexist and racist rhetoric on the international stage, the chances seemed slim. Nevertheless, Istanbul's bid seems somewhat precarious now too with the political demonstrations in full swing there. It is a hard one to call at the moment.

Finally, Ōya Minoru-sensei, kendo instructor at the International Budo University and long-time supporter of *Kendo World*, passed the first round of the 8-dan test recently in Kyoto. That in itself is no mean feat with a pass rate of less than 10%. So close... Ōya-sensei's book, *Reidan Jichi*, is being translated in instalments in *Kendo World* (part 15 on *kihon-dōsa* appears in this issue). KW wishes Ōya-sensei the best of luck and hopes that he is successful next time.

As always, *Kendo World* would like to receive reports of seminars and competitions that you have organised or attended, or other budo related matters. Please email your submissions to submissions@kendo-world.com. Thank you for your continued support.

The Kiwada Daiki Interview

By Blake Bennett

It is doubtful that there are many people who get a pleasant feeling when walking through the hallowed halls of the Osaka Police training centre. Perhaps it is only the kendo, judo, or *taiho-jutsu* sensei who manage to walk the corridors all smiles. After all, they are the only ones who know how hard today's training will be. Nevertheless, a reporter must make ballsy sacrifices when an opportunity arises to get some one-on-one interview time with the current All Japan Kendo Champion, and all-round good bloke, Kiwada Daiki. And so, there I was, signing in at the Osaka Police front office.

To set the scene, *Kendo World* was escorted up five flights of stairs (they seem to have a healthy policy of no elevators at the Osaka Police) and down a long, solemn corridor lined with a succession of 10-bed bunk rooms. Somewhat hospital-like in smell, it became clear that this was a building set up for *gasshuku*—probably the kind of *gasshuku* that makes you reconsider your decision to do kendo. I can only imagine the harshness experienced by the past and future champions that have stayed in these rooms, too exhausted to sleep. But not to worry, today I am here for a nice cup of coffee and a chat.

We take a seat at the front of a large, empty classroom, and with a list of questions that you, the reader requested, we begin the interview…

Kendo World: Thank you for taking the time to talk with me today.

Kiwada: No problem.

KW: Let me get straight to the point. How did you feel when you were crowned All Japan Champion?

Kiwada: Well, I think it was more a sense of relief than a feeling of elation. I know that if I were a bit younger, I would have been ecstatic. But as I get a little older my sense of duty to Japan and Japanese kendo has become a lot deeper. So while I was really happy to have realised my dream, it felt more like I had finally reached the start-line for my preparations for the next World Kendo Championship (WKC) as a Japanese representative.

KW: What is the pressure like having to win all the time?

Kiwada: Certainly, being watched by so many people can be quite a lot of pressure. But, in saying that there are definitely cases where the pressure actually helps me to perform. To be honest, the bigger the *taikai* is, the better I am able to use the pressure as strength, you know, to my advantage. At the WKC and the All Japan Kendo Championships (AJKC), I am much better at turning the pressure into motivation to perform well. Strangely enough, I find myself feeling much more nervous at smaller *shiai*…

KW: You are a complicated man then?!

Kiwada: I am, yeah! (Laughs)

KW: Are you more nervous at the AJKC, or the WKC?

Kiwada: Definitely the WKC! To me there is less of a feeling of obligation at the AJKC. If you lose, you have only let yourself down, and if you win it's only really you and your entourage who are really stoked. The WKC is a different story! You have the weight of the whole country on your shoulders…and I think that pressure is now more than ever.

KW: What sort of pressure do you feel going into the next AJKC?

Kiwada: I am just focusing on getting through the first couple of rounds for now! Those guys are going to make me work for it too! (Laughs)

KW: Do you have slumps?

Kiwada: Yes, of course.

KW: How do you overcome them?

Kiwada: Well, I like to have a broad range of techniques that I can use when I fight. So, for example, if I'm not having much luck with my *men* strikes, I will focus more on my *kote* attacks, or try more *hiki-waza*, or aim to score with *kaeshi-waza*. So, I guess, rather than trying to break through the wall in front of me, I try and find ways around it…

KW: How do you prepare for *shiai*?

Kiwada: I really put a lot of effort on managing my ideal body weight. Knowing what my best weight is, and not pushing over that number. Obviously training is paramount too. Before a *taikai* I will concentrate on short, sharp *kakari-geiko* type exercises. Things that get the heart rate going. I don't do a lot of long, drawn out *kihon* or anything like that, all that sort of thing should have been taken care of by then. You need to know your body can move quickly before *shiai*.

KW: So, how long prior to the event do you do the short, sharp *kakari-geiko*?

Kiwada: I would say from about two weeks out, until 3-4 days before…just going hard to get the body moving.

KW: How many kendo related injuries have you had?

Kiwada: Personally I have had two operations on my right elbow. I used to overdo the movement in my right arm and it caused some complications…a lot like tennis elbow, I guess you could say. So I have had to make some changes there. Other than that, I have never had any serious issues with my legs.

KW: Do you compliment your kendo training with weight-lifting exercises? If so, which exercises and why?

Kiwada: No, I don't do any weight training as part of my program. Anything that I do in the gym is focused on my core and back muscles. Weights training tends to build bulky muscles in the chest and arms that hamper the ability to take *kamae* properly. So I think it's better to concentrate on *suburi* and *suriashi* to develop muscles more specific to kendo.

KW: After a long day of hard training, what is your favourite drink?

Kiwada: I might get in trouble if I mention a certain beverage…so I guess I better say 'Pocari Sweat'… (laughs). Actually, we are really encouraged to drink sports drinks at the Japanese team squad training camps. Usually a watered down version of one-part sports drink, one-part water. That seems to be the best mix for the body after a tough training.

KW: What is your favourite food?

Kiwada: Ramen. Oh, and curry.
KW: What about curry ramen?
Kiwada: Nah, just ramen, or curry! (Laughs)
KW: Have you ever felt like quitting kendo?
Kiwada: Hmmm, yeah, in a sense I have…
KW: Why didn't you?
Kiwada: Well, I think you have to consider the difference between wanting to quit as a youngster, and wanting to pack it in now. For instance, as a kid, trainings are hard and you don't want to go to the dojo. Sometimes you get to the point where you just want to move on and try something else. But as an adult, say for example competing at the World Champs, I do find myself getting tired of the competition element sometimes. It's not a case of wanting to give up kendo per se, more like a desire to retire from *shiai*. In any case, I don't have the option to quit kendo! But yeah, I do sometimes feel after such a long time of competing, that I look forward to retiring from that side of it all…
KW: What or who is your greatest inspiration?
Kiwada: Now, my biggest motivation is preparing for the next WKC. That really inspires me to keep pushing. As far as inspiring people, I would have to say Teramoto Shōji-san and Takanabe Susumu-san. These two guys have really influenced me as a competitor. Of course there are many sensei and other people as well, but in terms of inspirations in my immediate surroundings, I would have to say them for sure.
KW: What do you think are the qualities that make up a champion?
Kiwada: That's a difficult one…I think that effort is a given. But I also think that effort alone is not enough. What is important, I think, is effort together with inspiration and creativity. Those three things are really crucial to success. So for example, an inventor has to put a lot of effort into his research, but he also needs inspiration to figure out what is necessary for the next step. And then, making use of that inspiration will take creativity to work out the 'how to'. Then again, effort is needed to stick at it no matter what… So, I think these three factors need to be repeated over and over in order to be successful at what you do…
KW: What are your impressions of international kendo?
Kiwada: From my experiences at the WKC, and also my time abroad teaching and training kendo, I think there has been a real step up in level overall. It's not just Korea anymore, there are parts of Europe, and of course America that have become real forces to be reckoned with. There is a genuine love of kendo and Japanese culture out there, and as people look to us to set an example, we have to really consider and sometimes reconsider the way that we conduct ourselves as Japanese kendo competitors. So in that way, I think we can learn a lot from the international kendo community as well.
KW: What are your five year goals?
Kiwada: In five years from now, I doubt I will be competing as I am now, so I think more of my focus will be on helping my juniors develop. In five years from now we'll be looking towards preparation for the 17th WKC, so I think I will have a big responsibility nurturing the kendo of the young guys heading into that campaign, and the young guys coming into the Osaka Police.
KW: Kiwada-san, thank you so much for your time this morning.
Kiwada: It was my pleasure. With that we went to lunch…

Over pasta, Kiwada-san tells me that his job as a policeman always takes precedence—that is to say, he is an officer of the law before he is a kendoka. Still, kendo trainings are a core part of the training regime for these men—with a menu which we all know must be gruelling. The natural result of all this are highly tuned *kenshi* who spend most of their waking moments breathing kendo, and are always on call and ready to serve their community.

A nice morning spent with a perfect gentleman, in one of the scariest kendo places in Japan.

HANSHI SAYS

A series in which some of Japan's top Hanshi teachers give hints of what they are looking for in grading examinations based on wisdom accumulated through decades of training.

AOKI HIKOTO (HANSHI 8-DAN)

Translated by Alex Bennett - *Kendo World* would like to thank Iizuka-sensei and *Kendo Jidai* Magazine for permission to translate and publish this article.

Aoki-sensei was born in 1937 in Oita prefecture. After graduating from Oita University, he entered the Oita Police Department, retiring from there in 1996. During his career, he competed successfully at the police championships, the National Sports Meet, the All Japan Kendo Championships and so on. He holds posts in the Oita prefecture Kendo Federation, and is the honorary Shihan of Oita Police Kendo. He passed the 8-dan examination in 1987, and received the title of Hanshi in 1995.

"Have you cultivated your overall capacity?"

I would like to start by explaining the attitude you should have towards promotion examinations. The purpose for attempting an examination in kendo is to establish your true level. There are no guarantees in examinations, and even people thought to possess the requisite skills for a particular grade may fail the test. Contrarily, some people who are not thought to be good enough may be successful in their examination. This is because there are other factors involved other than just skill level. The kendo practitioner must persevere until they are successful.

A successful candidate will naturally come to possess the expected strength and grace for their grade, and those who do not pass will keep trying until they do. In this sense, examinations provide the kendo practitioner with a wonderful opportunity for improvement. Examinations reveal the true depth of kendo, and by undergoing the rigorous training process in the quest to pass a given grade, the kendo practitioner firms his or her resolve, and purifies their kendo. Therefore, in order to pass an examination, it is critical that the practitioner cultivates their "overall capacity".

Anyone who is fortunate in their training environment will be able to receive advice and guidance from their teachers and seniors in the course of their daily training. However, depending on one's work situation or location, ready access to such advice or training may not be possible. I suspect that most people fall into the latter category. It is essential for people in this situation to strive to improve their overall capacity.

That is to say, *keiko* is not just a matter of putting on *bōgu* and hitting your opponent. It means contemplating what you can do to improve all aspects of your kendo right now, and putting thought into action. This could entail jogging, walking, *suburi*, reading instructional books, or anything to this effect. It requires a belief that whatever you do is for the benefit of your overall capacity, and sparing no effort to this end. By doing this, kendo will become inextricably connected with your daily life. You will be able to overcome various difficulties in your work, and in turn, this experience will benefit your kendo.

"*Seme* with your *ki*, *seme* with your sword, *seme* with your body…"

Next, I will outline three decisive points for passing. It goes without saying that you have to outshine your opponent to pass an examination. In order to do this, you need to strike your opponent. Even if other areas are superior to your opponent, if you are unable to land successful attacks, you will not be able to pass. To strike successfully in kendo is based on how you "*seme*" (apply pressure) and "*tame*" (hold), and how you take advantage of openings. Use your *ki*, sword, and body to comprehensively apply *seme* on your opponent. Consolidating these three factors in your *seme* is called "*sankō-itchi*" (unification of three attacks).

First, what is *seme* by *ki*? It is said the body is permeated with *ki*, or energy. The rigidity in your shoulders will dissipate by putting tension in your lower-abdomen, imagining it is an inflated balloon. In other words, when in *kamae*, ideally the upper body is "empty" while the lower body is "replete", and this is the condition you need to be in to confront and apply pressure on your opponent.

There is an old teaching that says, "If you grip the hilt too strongly, your *ki* will not transmit to the tip of the sword." You should aim for *ki* to surge through your body from your gut, and for your *kiai* to be diffused through to the *kensen*. Just like a deep and powerful lion's roar, your *kiai* should emanate from your lower abdomen. There is a saying in Japanese, "*me ni mono wo miseru*". Literally translated as "show something to their eyes", it means to teach somebody a lesson, or to show somebody a thing or two. This determination lies at the basis of a fight or match. To take advantage of an opening or weakness requires recognition of the opponent's condition, to observe the them with total concentration and clarity. In order to "show something to their eyes", you have to be able to use your own first. Furthermore, when applying pressure with *ki*, you must show conviction in your attack (*sutemi*), and not be concerned with winning or losing, or having a strong desire to strike but to not be struck. You must let go when you face your opponent, or else openings will also manifest in your kendo.

Next, what is *seme* with the sword? This refers to applying pressure through the tip of the sword (*kissaki* or *kensen*), and pressurising your opponent by striking. Another old teaching contends "The power of life and death is within 9cm of the *kissaki*". Famous sword masters of the past have also referred to the importance of the *kensen*. For example, "Fire springs from the *kensen*" (Terada Muneari), "A ring of flames arises from the *kensen*" (Shirai Tōru), and "The *kensen* gradually gets bigger and bigger" (Yamaoka Tesshū). Also, "The *kissaki* should be used to lift the sword, and to cut. If *ki* crosses into the tip of the sword, it will carry the blade."

As these teachings suggest, it is the movement of the *kensen* that determines the fight. So, how should the *kensen* be used to apply *seme*?

1. *Seme* by keeping the *kensen* on the opponent's centreline.
2. *Seme* by changing the direction the *kensen* is pointing.

The opponent's *kamae* will become unsettled if you use your wrists well (flexibly) and shift your *kensen* up, down, left and right. This is referred to as "*seme happō*" (eight directions of *seme*).
3. Unsettle your opponent's *kamae* by sweeping, holding down, twisting, slapping, and knocking their *shinai* down.
4. Striking action. For example, apply pressure to your opponent's *kote*, and when they try to defend it, strike *men*. Also, an opening in created when the opponent tries to block or move away from your attack. This is also applying *seme* with the sword.

How does one apply pressure with the body? When you move in towards your opponent, he or she will think your intention is to strike, and will feel under pressure. If the act of attacking and defending *maai* – the spatial distance between you and your opponent – is compared with attacking a castle, the point at which the two *kissaki* come into contact is like attacking the outer moat. You have to get past the moat and fight up to the castle gates (the opponent's hands). Their *kamae* will be unsettled by this point, and then you can attack the castle tower (*men*). This process requires advancing the whole body.

Harigaya Sekiun left the following teaching. "Generally, when assailing an enemy with your sword, if you are too far away to attack, you should move in to a distance that is reachable. When you arrive, cut. If you are already at a closer interval, just cut from there. There is no need to think about it."

In order to strike, first you must break through to the appropriate distance. Even if you only shorten the distance a little, there will be a point where the opponent will be forced to change. This is the edge of the striking interval, and it is important to be the one to take the initiative and break through. "*Seme* feet" are vital in achieving this. The right foot is used to advance towards the opponent, but the left foot is immediately snapped into place behind it. *Seme* with the body must be executed with *seme* feet.

"Are you striking at the right opportunities?"

With regards to "*tame*", "If you do not have enough *tame* you will be too eager (*kioi*). If you have too much *tame*, you will become stationary (*itsuki*). *Tame* is not a matter of time. *Tame* is found between being too eager and being stationary." This was taught to me by my sensei, H8-dan Okada Shigemasa. Having *tame* is to be patient, but ready to pounce. If you apply *seme* with *sankō-itchi*, the opponent will prepare for your impending attack. If you follow through straight away, you will be blocked or countered. You must *seme* and also have *tame*, waiting for your opponent to react, build the pressure and then unleash the strike. This is to strike at the right opportunity. Thus, *tame* also means to probe for the right instant to attack. The opportunity, is also called "*ki*" (機) but uses a different *kanji* to *ki* for spirit (気). It arises as soon as there is a change in the opponent's mind, body, or technique.

From here, I will introduce some teachings that elucidate the meaning of *ki*: "*Sekka no ki*" (The moment flint stones spark) – When your *kiai* is sufficient and you are totally focused, you will be able to defeat your opponent the instant an opportunity arises, as quick as the gap between a flint being struck and the ensuing spark. Chiba Shūsaku talked of "*tsuyu no kurai*" (Dew dripping from a leaf).

> "If there is due on the leaves of a tree, they will fall to the ground as soon as you touch the branch. In the same way, in the art of *kenjutsu* you must be ready to pounce as soon as there is movement in the enemy's mind, technique, or body."

Yamaoka Tesshū taught that "*shinsei no shō*" (genuine victory) is gained by allowing the enemy to attack.

> "When two swordsmen face off with swords in hand, there is nobody who does not desire to go in and cut the other down. Therefore, resign yourself to allowing your enemy to succumb to this temptation, and when they launch their attack, use this opportunity to cut them first. This is genuine victory."

As all of these teachings suggest, the opportunity for attacking comes just as changes are occurring in the opponent. However, I would add that just striking is not sufficient. The attack must be made in adherence to correct *kihon* or fundamental movements. "*Ki*" (機) means openings for striking. Openings all emanate from the mind/heart. So, Yamaoka Tesshū is advising that the swordsman does not get gulled into desiring to strike, and wanting not to be struck. This makes a lot of sense, as such preoccupations cloud the mind. There is another teaching that the "*Kamae* and the heart are essentially the same". This means that if the heart moves or is disturbed, so too will be the *kamae*. This notion is often mentioned in kendo using terms such as *shikai* (four sicknesses of the mind – surprise, fear, doubt, and hesitation), and the aforementioned "eagerness" (*kioi*) to strike, or being unable to move (*itsuki*). Ultimately in kendo, you must "use the heart to strike at the heart". This should be aspired to in the course of your every day training, and represents the boundless depth of kendo.

"Are your strikes technically correct?"

Striking in a technically correct fashion is based on the following important considerations: first, your striking form should be in accordance with proper *kihon* movements. Understand the importance of *uchikomi-geiko*, and make every effort to expunge bad habits or quirks you may have developed. Second, your strikes should "cut", and be powerful. Use the left hand to manipulate the *shinai* with an ample swing, and then use the same left hand to make the strike. Avoid putting too much power in the grip of the right hand at the instant of impact on the target. Third, know how to use both hands in the strike. Be cognizant of the roles of the left hand and right hands when striking.

The left hand is the lifting hand, the striking hand, and the stopping hand (your left hand stops firmly at chest height). The right hand is like the "rudder", helping the left hand navigate towards the target. It is also the "protector hand" used to invalidate the opponent's attacks, and to push or move the body out of the way. The right hand is also the "deflection hand" used for executing techniques such as *suriage-waza* and *kaeshi-waza*.

H9-dan Matsumoto Toshio-sensei called this important skill as "striking with the wrists". He taught the following important points for using the hands effectively when striking:

1. You first need a good understanding of proper *tenouchi* (way of gripping the *shinai*) before you can strike properly, utilising the wrists to good effect. In other words, the *shinai* should be swung with the wrists.
2. The *shinai* should start moving from the wrist joint of the left hand. When the strike is made, the left hand should stop at chest height.
3. When starting the striking movement with the left hand, imagine that there is a spring at the bottom of your hand. As the striking hand advances into the swing, the springs becomes tighter, and then recoils back with incredible force as the strike is made onto the target.
4. If the left hand is held in a position that is too low in the *kamae*, there will not be enough room to move in the way mentioned above in 3. Therefore, the swing will be smaller, and the strike will be weak and ineffectual, merely "tapping" the target rather than cutting it.

These are the main points I assess when serving as an examiner at gradings. In short, *seme* → *tame* → technical correctness in the strike.

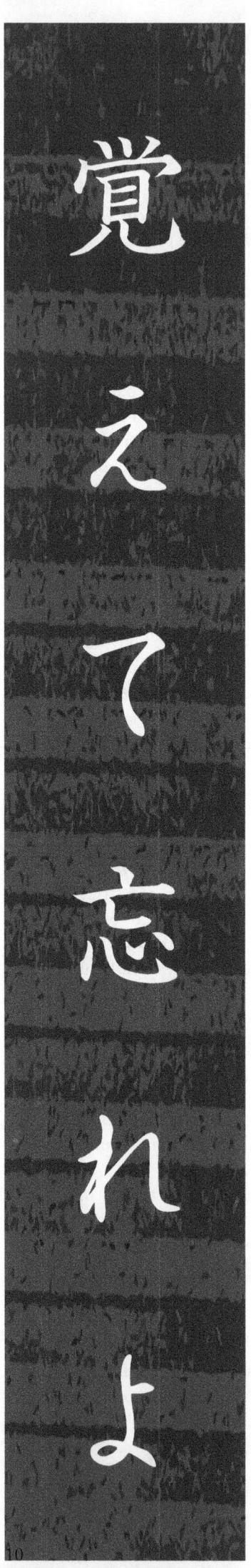

"Remember, then forget"

Hōzōin In'ei (1521–1607)
Founder of the Hōzōin-ryū Sōjutsu school of spearmanship.

Hōzōin In'ei was a Buddhist monk of the Kōfuku-ji temple in Nara. He was not a warrior per se, but was still a master of the warrior arts. The Kōfuku-ji maintained around forty temples in Nara, of which In'ei oversaw the Hōzōin. But it was because of his sublime skills in the martial arts that he was to become immortalised. Apart from the important position as the guardian of the Hōzōin temple in the ancient capital of Nara, In'ei also founded what became an immensely prominent school of *sōjutsu* (spearmanship) known as the Hōzōin-ryū. Peaceful Buddhism and martial arts perhaps do not seem like such a probable mix, but in fact Japanese temples have a violent history, and actively participated in uprisings and wars. Nara's monks had long revered the martial arts, and were certainly not pushovers in a fight.

In'ei was a dedicated aficionado of the martial arts. He studied the Nen-ryū under Toda Yosaemon. He also studied the Katori Shinto-ryū under the legendary Iizasa Chōisai Ienao. In fact, it was In'ei who apparently set up the fateful meeting between two more great swordsmen Kamiizumi Ise-no-Kami Nobutsuna and Yagyū Sekishusai Muneyoshi. He was also mentored by Daizendayū Moritada in spear skills. Old documents of the school record how, one evening, he saw a reflection of the moon on Sarusawa pond. The image inspired him to create a new kind of spear with crescent-shaped hook fixed at right angles to the shaft. It is known as the *jūmonji-yari*. As the old saying goes, "It can be a spear to thrust. It can be a *naginata* to cleave. It can be a *kama* to slash. In any case, it never fails to hit the target."

He received many hints for combat from his warrior acquaintances. He was particularly friendly with Yagyū Muneyoshi, and it seems that he provided

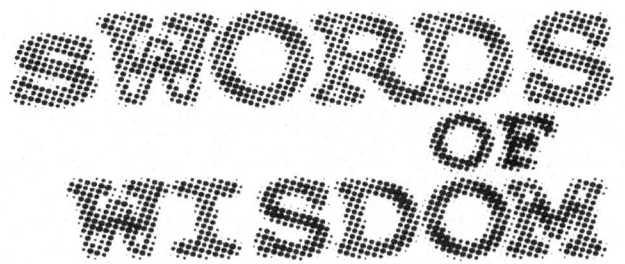

By
ALEX BENNETT
Based on the book
"KENSHI NO MEIGON" (1998)
by the late Tobe Shinjūrō
Used with author's permission.

some of the important fundamental knowledge for the Hōzōin-ryū when In'ei formed it. During his career he defeated (=probably killed) 12 sword masters, and made quite a name for himself throughout the land. However, feeling pangs of guilt from taking life – an act that ran counter to the tenets of Buddhism – he lay down his *yari* and passed on the reins of the school to his top disciple Nakamura Ichiuemon (1577–1652) and others, and then went into retirement. In'ei died at the age of 86 in 1607.

Such was the reputation of the monks, that even the amazing Miyamoto Musashi ventured into Nara to test his skills against adept of the Hōzōin-ryū. He did not encounter In'ei, but instead fought Okuzōin, a monk who lived in the neighbourhood. According to the *Nitenki*, Musashi won easily against the monk. Perhaps the school's techniques had deteriorated by this time, or maybe Musashi was genuinely just too damned good.

There was another renowned warrior of the Warring States period called Kani Saizō (1554–1613). He eventually came to serve under Fukushima Masanori when Japan finally entered an era of peace, but he was very much a man of yesteryear. His exploits in battle were celebrated, and he collected heads like most people do stamps. With too many to carry back in one battle, he placed bamboo grass in the mouths of his fallen foe to identify his kills at a more convenient time.

He was skilled at using the spear, and in his later years he was challenged by a young warrior to a match. He complied, but dressed himself and his horse up in armour as if he was heading to the front rather than engaging in a singular bout. The young warrior was somewhat surprised. "All I wanted was a one-on-one match." Saizō replied, "LOL! This is how I always fight my one-on-one matches!" Maybe his concept of a "match" was truly life and death combat, or he just wanted to re-enact the good old days.

In any case, Saizō knew well of In'ei's reputation, and in his younger days he went looking for him in Nara. "I hear that you established your own school of spearmanship. I want to learn the secrets." In'ei responded, "There are no great secrets as such. We have *jōdan* upper stance, *chūdan* middle stance, and lift the weapon overhead. Then we just go nuts…"

Still, Saizō wanted to learn. Given his actual combat experience, he was a gifted and strong student. But when it came time to test his new spear skills in battle, he found he could not move. He was not scared at all, but found his body would not do what his mind wanted, and the tips of his enemy's spears were particularly perturbing. He went back and asked In'ei what he thought could be wrong. "You are too raw. You need to train more and stop thinking so much."

He continued to train hard, and then went back into the fray. He wasn't as hesitant as before, but his movement was still impeded. Again, he went to see his master in Nara. "You mustn't be preoccupied with spear techniques. If anything, you should try and forget everything once you have learned it…"

Saizō then had an epiphany. Before he started learning Hōzōin techniques, he was able to attack unreservedly with *mushin*, or no-mind. It was natural and effective. The secret that he learned from In'ei was quite simply to "learn, and then forget." The techniques should become a natural manifestation of movement in battle, rather than rigidly adhering to some contrived form. He was back in business.

THE NUTS 'N' BOLTS OF KENDO

By Nakano Yasoji, (Kendo Hanshi 9-dan)   Translated by Alex Bennett

EFFECTIVE TRAINING METHODS—KIRIKAESHI

KIRIKAESHI HAS LONG BEEN A STAPLE TRAINING EXERCISE IN KENDO. PLEASE EXPLAIN THE BEST WAY TO DO IT.

I think that there are three points in particular that need attention. The first is breathing. After making the first *men* strike, you should take a deep breath and do consecutive *men* strikes with one breath. Many people are prone to make each strike with a single breath. This is the wrong way of going about it. Consecutive strikes moving forwards and then backwards should be all made in the same breath, and then finish the final cut also in the same breath.

Then there is the issue of the angle of the blade when striking. Many people make their strikes widely from each side. Again, this is wrong. The left hand should never veer away from the centreline of the body. If the left hand alternates from left to right with each strike, your technique will not develop and the entire exercise will be futile. The left hand moves up and down the centre axis, and the *shinai* should be turned each time to ensure that the blade is on the correct cutting angle for each side. The striking distance is also very important. Maintain a distance that is relative to the receiver to guarantee that the *monouchi* part of the *shinai* strikes the left and right *men* accurately.

Chiba Shūsaku, the famous swordsman of the Tokugawa period (1603–1868), relayed the following important points with regards to *kirikaeshi*:

TEN POINTS FOR THE STRIKER

1) The striking should be spirited and gradually become more rapid.
2) The strikes should be powerful.
3) Make your breath last as long as possible.
4) The arms should be unrestricted in movement.
5) The body should move lightly and adroitly.
6) *Shinai* of longer length should be able to be wielded without stinting.
7) The lower body should be stable, with core power focused in the abdomen.
8) The eyes should be sharp.
9) Maintain the correct striking distance.
10) Be sure that the *tenouchi* (grip) is flexible, and each strike resonates.

EIGHT POINTS FOR THE RECEIVER

1) Be calm.
2) The eyes should be sharp.
3) Observe the flight of each strike carefully.
4) Body movement should be effortless.
5) The body should be stable and steady.
6) The *tenouchi* should be firm.
7) Block each strike cleanly.
8) Build up the strength in your arms.

THERE ARE TWO MAIN METHODS FOR RECEIVING IN KIRIKAESHI: HOLDING THE SHINAI IN A VERTICAL POSITION AND BLOCKING EACH STRIKE ALTERNATELY ON THE LEFT AND RIGHT SIDE OF THE BODY; AND KEEPING THE LEFT HAND IN THE CENTRE OF THE BODY WHILE HITTING DOWN EACH MEN STRIKE. WHAT IS THE BEST WAY FOR RECEIVING?

There are many methods for receiving *kirikaeshi*, and just as many justifications for each. I heard from H10-dan Mochida Moriji-sensei that when receiving alternately on each side of the body, the left hand should move no more than 10cm. He also said it is best to receive each strike with a *suri-otoshi* movement (sliding hit-down). When receiving for beginners, do so by pulling your own *shinai* back a little to encourage the strikes to extend out further. For stronger hitters, *suri-otoshi* is useful to help them learn to regulate their striking power.

WE OFTEN HEAR ABOUT HOW CENTRAL KIRIKAESHI WAS IN TRAINING IN THE OLD DAYS. OLDER SENSEI RECOUNT THEIR YOUTH IN WHICH ALL THEY DID WAS KIRIKAESHI AND NOTHING ELSE. WAS THIS THE CASE, AND IF SO, WAS IT NOT A LITTLE EXCESSIVE?

Actually, when I was student at the Tokyo Higher Normal School, we didn't do a lot of *kirikaeshi* to tell the truth. I'm not saying that this was a good thing, but we often went straight into *ji-geiko*. We didn't do *kirikaeshi* excessively, as was the case in some other schools. Needless to say, there is no doubt that *kirikaeshi* is absolutely crucial for learning the basics, but only if it is done correctly. If your left hand strays from the centreline, or your strikes are small, or conducted in front of your body instead of overhead, then there really is no point to it.

REIDAN-JICHI PART 15

KIHON-DŌSA: No. 4

By Prof. Ōya Minoru (Kendo Kyōshi 7-dan)
International Budo University

Translated by Alex Bennett
Some sections of the text incorporate previous translations of Ōya-sensei's work by Steven Harwood

Kihon-dōsa, or basic movements, refers to *kamae*, footwork and the manipulation of the *shinai*. In other words, it entails all of the principles behind striking and thrusting movements for scoring *yūkō-datotsu* (valid attacks) in kendo.

Striking Basics

Jōge-buri and *naname-buri* lead into *kūkan-datotsu*, or accurate striking without hitting an actual target. This in turn extends to striking an opponent with *fumikomi-ashi* (stamping footwork) from *issoku-ittō-no-ma* (one-step, one-sword interval). This process represents the transition from *kihon-dōsa* (basic movements) to *taijin-ginō* (techniques against an opponent). In other words, *kihon-dōsa* encompasses the fundamental movements for striking *yūkō-datotsu*, or scoring a valid point against an opponent. Thus, although the actual movements seem simple, they must be perfected through repeated basic striking and *uchikomi-geiko*.

Through this process of "cutting air", the practitioner must improve the quality of his or her strikes by learning to synchronise footwork and *shinai* manipulation, and checking each aspect of the striking motion and content. In the initial stages, the practitioner can use *suri-ashi* (sliding footwork) rather than stamping on the strike to master the striking action first. After progress has been made, *fumikomi-ashi* (stamp) may be incorporated into the strike to make it more powerful and realistic.

The Theory behind the Striking Motion

The technical sequence starts with two practitioners facing off in *kamae* probing for opportunities to make valid strikes, followed by a demonstration of *zanshin* (continued physical and psychological alertness) after a strike is made. Regardless of how well a striking opportunity is seized, and an appropriate *waza* is initiated, if the striking motion is executed inadequately, it will never transpire into a valid attack. The main objective is to strike with correct *hasuji* (blade angle). This predicated by the precision of the motion in mid-flight, and preceding that, smooth commencement of the strike which stems from the *kamae*. After the strike is made, it must be "sealed", and then preparation made for the next attack. *Kamae* → Starting the strike → Mid-flight → Contact → (main objective) Seal it → Preparation…

Stage	Beginning →	Imaginary →	Singular Movement →	Practical
Technical Progression	Jōge/Naname-buri	Kūkan-datotsu	Kihon-datotsu	Taijin-ginō
Footwork	Suri-ashi	Suri-ashi → Fumikomi		Fumikomi
Shinai Manipulation	Big, precise, slow	Big, precise, sharp		

1. Kamae

See my previous articles on the finer points of assuming *kamae* correctly.

2. Kamae → Starting the strike

The strike commences by shifting the centre of gravity and moving forward from the right foot. At the same time, the grip of the left hand starts to move. The important thing to remember is, as the right foot and left hand start to move, activation of the left hip and the left leg that supports it thrusts the body forward. Pushing the left hip in the same direction as the *kensen* (towards the opponent) drives the centre of gravity forwards, and enables the right foot to advance smoothly. By moving the left hip in the direction of the *kensen* and advancing the right foot, the left hand also moves in the direction of the *kensen*. The whole movement is buoyed by the left leg.

the body will become unbalanced, and the strike will lack accuracy, becoming what is called a "right-handed strike". Moving the left hip in the direction of the *kensen* will enable the centre of gravity to shift forward, and the right foot and left hand will move at the same time. Thus, the movement of the centre of gravity enables the left hand and right hand to move at the simultaneously in a balanced movement. Also, moving the left hip and left hand in the same direction as the *kensen* facilitates a more powerful, focused strike utilising the entire body.

The *kamae* expedites smooth commencement of the striking movement. The right foot and hand are held in front of the body, and the *shinai* is gripped with both hands. The body has to move from a stationary but stable position without revealing any obvious preparatory movements. The movement is driven from within, which is why the striking action in kendo is so difficult.

3. Starting the Strike → Mid-flight

At this stage, the shoulders, elbows, and wrists must be flexible, and the *shinai* is directed decisively towards the target.

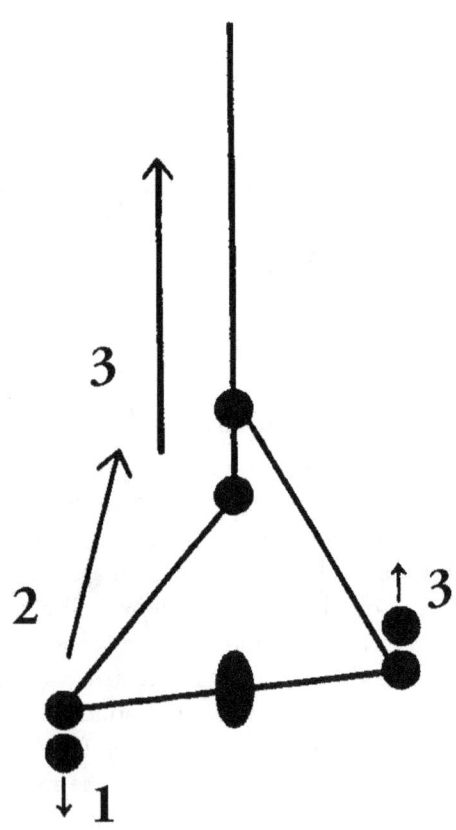

1. Left leg propping the body
2. Left hip moves in the same direction as the *kensen*
3. The right foot advances smoothly
3. The left hand moves in the same direction as the *kensen* (at same time)

Considerations

In *chūdan-no-kamae*, the right hand and right foot are positioned in front of the body. However, if only the front limbs are extended out to complete the attack,

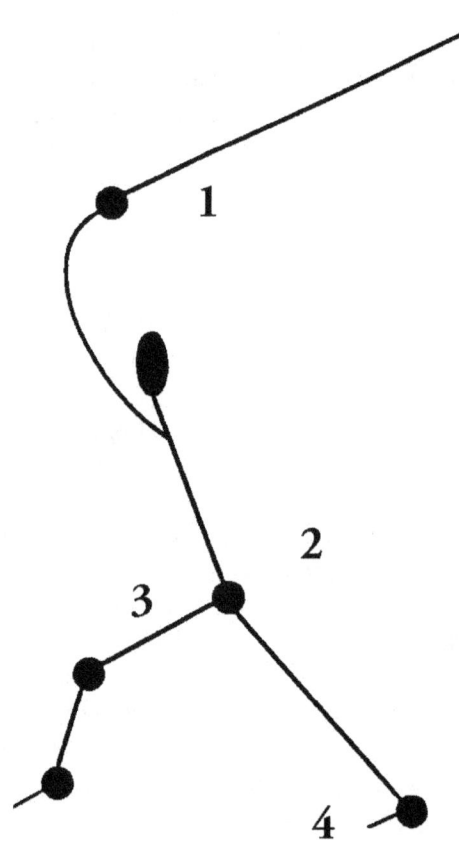

1 Keeping the joints of the arms supple, the *shinai* is lifted up and brought down to strike
2 The hips are stable throughout the movement
3 The right foot advances smoothly
4 The left leg supports the whole movement

Considerations

It is very important that the joints of the shoulders, elbows and wrists are kept supple throughout the start and striking actions. This will make the strike smooth but powerful. When hitting a nail with a hammer or beating a drum, you need to swing the hammer or drumstick adequately to drive the nail into the wood or make the drum reverberate. Kendo is the same. In order to make the strike count, the swing of the *shinai* must be sufficient.

The body is moved forward in the Starting the Strike→Mid-flight stage. How should the *shinai* be manipulated? The left fist is thrust forward in the same direction the *kensen* is pointing. This means that the *shinai* is swung up as the body advances directly towards the opponent.

If the attacker is only focused on striking quickly, the hands gripping the *shinai* will go straight to the target and the strike will be made without swinging up first – as in "*sashi-men*", which is more of a thrust than a cut. The resulting strike will be weak, and the angle of the blade will be incorrect. It is a great misapprehension to think that thrusting the left hand forward to generate a swing before striking is going to slow the attack motion down. As long as the wrists, elbows, and shoulders are kept flexible throughout the motion, the strike can be made in one swift movement.

Modern kendo entails using a bamboo *shinai* to strike at designated target points on the opponent's body by swinging it up and down. Whether the swing is large or small depends on various factors that arise during the engagement, such as the spatial interval between the two practitioners.

4. Mid-flight → Strike

If the shoulders, wrists, and elbows are flexible rather than rigid, the flight of the *shinai* will be smooth but powerful. Posture is kept upright and supported by the left leg as the right foot moves forward. The grip is tightened upon impact as the right foot stamps on the floor.

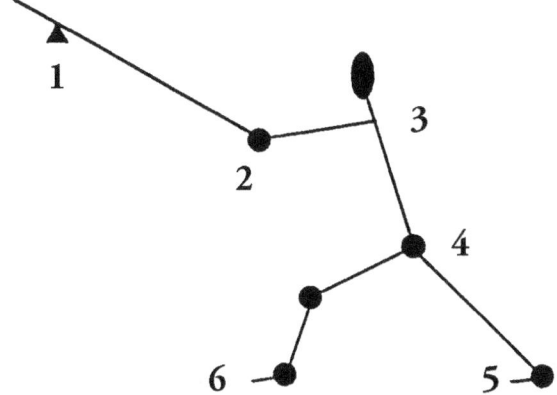

1. Correct blade angle
2. Tightening the grip
3. Upper body posture
4. Lower back stability
5. Left leg supports the body
6. Right foot stamp as the strike is made (*fumikomi*)

Considerations

The strike must be made with intent, otherwise it will be no more than a fluke if the *shinai* hits the target. For a strike to be considered valid, it must be executed in "full spirits" with "correct posture" and "proper blade angle" (*hasuji*) – with a consolidation of spirit, sword and body (*ki-ken-tai*). The grip needs to be tightened on impact to ensure the blade angle is correct. Also, the lower back area must be stable enough to keep the upper body straight throughout the attacking process. Furthermore, the left leg ensures that the lower back and hips are stable. If stability is not maintained, then the angle of the blade during the movement will be incorrect. In particular, if the left foot flies up at the back, this will result in an unbalanced posture, and incorrect striking techniques. The right foot (stamp or *fumikomi*) serves to "seal" the strike. However, it is the left foot and leg that is used to support and propel the body forward, so it can be considered as the "striking foot".

5. Strike → Seal

To seal the strike, the impact point where the *shinai* meets the target does not move as the left foot is snapped up behind the right in an important movement called *hikitsuke*. Left foot *hikitsuke* → hips pulled up → upper body is straightened → posture is rectified.

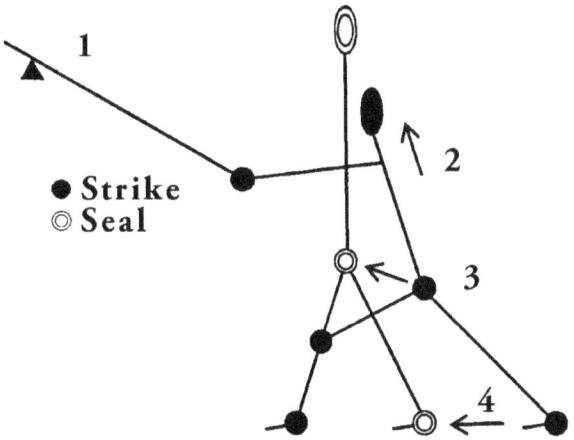

1. Strike point does not move
2. Upper body is straightened
3. Hips pulled up
4. Left foot snapped up

Considerations

To "seal" the strike means to ensure that it is decisive and finalised. After striking with "full spirits", this feeling continues to finish the process. The way in which the attack is vocalised is crucial. Rather than "*meeeeeeen!*", the ideal is "*mennnnnn!*" In other words, "*me*" is vocalised at the instant of the strike, and "*nnnnn*" as it is sealed by snapping up the left foot and correcting the upper body posture. Only then will the strike be decisive. If the left foot stays still or flies up at the back as the strike is made, posture will be compromised, and the strike will not be valid. The ability to "seal the strike" with all of these components is indicative of the quality and level of practitioner's kendo, and the sound of the strike as it is made will be crisp (*sae*).

6. Seal → Get ready again

The next step after sealing the strike is to readjust and get ready for the next. The *ki* or spirit is composed, and the body and sword return to the ready positions after following through. The footwork in the follow-through is *okuri-ashi*. The distance between the feet when running through after the strike becomes incrementally smaller by halves, and the steps become quicker. This means that the attacker will usually advance four or five steps after sealing the strike, coming to a stop at the right distance to turn and face off in *kamae*. During, and at the end of the follow-through, always be prepared mentally and physically to respond to any situation or counterattack from the opponent. This is *zanshin*.

7. Arms and Grip on the Shinai

Just as with hammering a nail into a piece of wood, or beating a drum, to gain enough power for a strike in kendo requires a swing to gain momentum first, and then focusing the power into the point of impact. The power for the strike is generated from the swing up and down as one movement. The use of the hands and grip (*tenouchi*) is fundamental for directing the power of the strike in the right direction. The manner of the grip is directly connected to whether or not the angle and direction of the blade in the strike is correct. Generally, as practitioners become more proficient, their swing transitions from big and strong, to small and sharp. In other words, use of the hands (*tenouchi*) becomes more advanced, and the practitioner is able to generate considerable power with smaller movements. This results in what is referred to as "*sae*", or crispness in the strike.

Furthermore, for the strike to be straight requires the power to be spread evenly between the left and right arms, with no extraneous strength. When the *shinai* is swung downwards, power transfers from the shoulders → elbows → wrists, from the centre to the extremities. The power then moves into the palms of the hands which holds the handle (*tsuka*) of the *shinai*, and the little finger, ring finger, and middle finger tighten in an instant which adds velocity to the *shinai*. It is this connected process of power transferral that results in a strike with *sae*.

If the wrists become rigid on impact, or conversely bend and show wrinkles, this is an indication that the power of the strike has stopped in the wrists, and will not be transferred to the *kensen* of the *shinai*. It is impossible to strike with *sae* in this case. Also, if the palms of the hands are facing upwards when the strike is made, this will inevitably result in the *shinai* merely being placed on the target, and again, it will not be a valid strike. It is important to utilise the tendons in the lower side of the forearms to bring the little, ring, and middle fingers on each hand into play, and tense them the instant contact with the target is made.

In my next article, I will analyse the striking actions for specific targets.

LOCKIE JACKSON

UNLOCKING Japan

PART 24 Gaijin Style

A thought provoking YouTube video recently hit my e-mail inbox. Under normal circumstances, my finger would have been over the delete button of this unsolicited piece of junk faster than the perfect *debana-kote*, but for reasons unbeknown to me, I actually opened it. Apparently, the thing had been doing the rounds among the expat community in Japan, and, by some accounts it had even gone 'viral'. Entitled "Gaijin Style", the clip was a spoof of the South Korean pop star Psy's internationally acclaimed song "Gangnam Style". Just as the neologism Gangnam Style refers to the trends, inclinations, and lifestyles of the well-heeled inhabitants of Seoul's Gangnam district, its parody "Gaijin Style" is a less-than-light-hearted mocking of the way many young, white, heterosexual men in Japan are often perceived to "piss away" the better years of their lives on the archipelago. The clip opens with a young man waking up on a park bench surrounded by empty beer cans. The third verse struck me as particularly curious:

I left my country so I didn't have to see another whitey,
But when it's time to pick up chicks I head right to Roppongi,
I tell girls I'm a banker or I manage funds at Barclay,
But I teach at McDonalds nightly.

Two dominant stereotypes of '*gaijin* guys' in Japan can easily be discerned from this. Sexist terminology aside, the first is the assertion that *gaijin* men are hypersexual maniacs who systematically prey on demure, unsuspecting, if not undiscerning, Japanese women. The second is that they have no respectable career to speak of – that they are unqualified moron's who find it hard to admit that they are – shock horror – lowly language teachers, even to themselves.

"I don't speak Japanese," the next verse refrains, "and when I'm on the train no one sits next to me." It is here that the vitriol towards *gaijin* men starts to get ramped up. "I'm loud and drunk and rude and I don't care who sees. I'm a rock star here but a loser in my own country!" Yes indeed, *gaijin* men are often portrayed as idiotic degenerates with vastly over-inflated opinions of their sexual, professional, and intellectual self-worth. I imagine more than the odd Japan-based reader is finding these paragraphs, at the very least, slightly self-confronting. "Could I be a *gaijin* loser?" I hear them ask themselves.

The clip reminded me of an earlier and somewhat more celebrated take on foreign men in Japan. *Charisma Man*, the creation of Writer Larry Rodney and illustrator Glen Schroeder, was a comic strip that originally ran in the now defunct expat magazine *The Alien*. In it, Charisma Man, a former geeky, weak, burger-flipping loser from Canada, is transformed into a chisel-chinned, womanising hunk when he comes to Japan to teach English. Like the Gaijin Style clip, the comic strip lampoons the way in which many unattractive, socially inept foreign men in Japan seem to be able to reinvent themselves in the playground that Japan is perceived to be.

Both the Gaijin Style clip, and the comic strip *Charisma Man*, got me mulling over two simple questions. Firstly, does Charisma Man actually exist? If one is of the opinion that some foreign men in Japan go through a stage where they behave arrogantly and narcissistically as they come to grips with their place in (or even outside) society here, then yes, I would say the negative stereotype of Charisma Man has, like most stereotypes, some basis of fact. A stroll through any one of the countless Roppongi or Shinsaibashi bars any night of the week will bear evidence of this. But could this not be said of almost any entertainment district around the world? My view is that most foreign guys in Japan temporarily display at least some traits of Charisma Man as they wrestle and come to terms with the living-in-Japan experience. For the fortunate, the process might be called 'growing up'. For the less so, 'arrested development'.

I would also be willing to admit that many of the foreign guys in my circle of friends are, to put it diplomatically, a little bit quirky. I can't think of a single mate of mine who could be described as fashionable (sorry guys). I'll admit to being a bit of a dork growing up in Australia, and I reckon pretty much all of the guys on the *Kendo World* team are a little bit strange (again, sorry guys). [Editors Note: People in glass houses should not throw stones, Dr. Jackson] Perhaps one has to be to live here for any great length of time. Some are in lines of work that they perhaps would not have – or have had to – pursue if they had stayed in their own country. Does that make them 'losers'? I guess that depends on what you think a 'winner' is.

To me, *gaijin* style is about being comfortable in your own skin living in Japan. It's about completely embracing the things you love about the place, and rejecting the cultural or ideological elements that don't sit comfortably with who you understand yourself to be. Some would disapprovingly call this attitude cherry-picking, but I have never thought that my ability to live a productive, enjoyable life in Japan was a zero-sum game.

The 43rd Kanagawa-ken Yonsha Taikō Kendo Taikai

By Michael Ishimatsu-Prime

On Sunday February 17, 2013, the Kanagawa Prefectural Budokan in Yokohama hosted the "43rd Kanagawa-ken Yonsha Taikō Kendo Taikai" (the 43rd Kanagawa Prefecture Four Team Kendo Competition) in which four 15-member teams represented the prefecture's police, teachers, company workers and university students. They competed against each other in a league, in four-minute, *sanbon-shōbu* bouts. Of the 15 members of each team, the Senpō and Jihō were female.

As the police team is made up of *tokuren*, who are essentially professional kendoka, they are the perennial favourites. They have lived up to that reputation by winning the preceding 42 competitions, but the teachers have come close once. They beat the police but then lost against the students which gifted the championship, once again, to the police. This year, would the police make it 43 times in a row? They were under the watchful eye of Miyazaki Fumihiro-sensei and Takanabe Susumu, two-time All Japan Champion.

The teachers were a mix of junior and senior high school teachers, as well as a solitary elementary school teacher, but surprisingly there were no university teachers. One teacher who I had hoped to see was Asahina Kazuo, a former member of the Kanagawa *tokuren* who quit the police in April 2012 to become a teacher at Yamato Higashi High School. He was the surprise package of the 2012 AJKC, making it to the best eight, but losing to Tokyo's Uchimura Ryōichi.

However, Asahina unfortunately did not take part in this competition.

The students are selected for the team based on competition results throughout the year. There are a few strong kendo universities in Kanagawa such as Tokai University and Kanagawa University from which the students were selected.

The company worker's team was made up of representatives from well-known companies like Fuji Film, Fujitsu, and Hitachi, as well as a railway company, bank, furniture store and trading company. The majority of the company workers were 4-dan, with three 5-dan and 3-dan each.

Not surprisingly, it was the police who were the first to arrive and start their warm-up. Everybody in the Budokan, spectators and competitors alike, intently watched their routine which included lots of *suburi*, followed by *kirikaeshi* and *kihon-waza*. Once that had finished, they all gathered around their sensei for a last minute pep-talk. This was in stark contrast to the teachers, who seemed to be enjoying themselves and appeared more relaxed than any other team. The students were the last to turn up.

The action took place on two *shiai-jō*. First up on Court 1 was the police against the company workers. The first two matches ended in a draw with no *ippon* scored, followed by a victory for the police, and another draw. Of the remaining 11 matches, the police lost

Match Results

	Police	Company Workers	Teachers	Students	Matches Won	Bouts Won	Ippon Scored	Ranking
Police		○ 16/11	○ 14/8	○ 15/8	3	27	45	1
Company Workers	△ 3/1		△ 9/3	△ 10/3	0	7	22	4
Teachers	△ 6/2	○ 11/3		○ 12/8	2	13	29	2
Students	△ 3/1	○ 13/5	△ 4/2		1	8	20	3

Ranking:
1st Police
2nd Teachers
3rd Students
4th Company Workers

one and won the rest, conceding only two *ippon* in the process. They finished 11-1 winners.

On Court 2 it was the teachers versus students, and after five matches, it was tied at 2-2. Three draws followed before the teachers found their groove and ended up winning all but one of the final seven matches to finish 8-2.

After a break of only a few minutes, the second round of matches got under way. The teachers versus company workers was a very close match ending 3-3. The teachers were declared winners as they had scored the greater number of *ippon* – 11 to the company workers' nine.

While that match was going on, all eyes were fixed on Court 1 where the police were fighting the students. For a while, it looked like the students might be able to pull off an upset. They won their first match with two good *men* strikes, and the next four ended in hard-fought draws with no *ippon*. It took the police until the sixth match before they were able to get their first *ippon* and victory, and from there, they took control. Of the remaining ten matches, there were another two scoreless draws, and the police only conceded one *ippon*, and took two *ippon* in all but two matches to finish up 8-1 winners.

Before the final two matches began, both the company workers and students were looking for their first victory, and were playing for third place. Also, the police and teachers were tied at two wins each, so whoever won would win the competition.

On Court 2, the students and company workers match was close. After 12 bouts, the students were in the lead by a narrow margin of 3-2. They also had a slight lead of 9-7 in the number of *ippon* scored. For the company workers to be sure of victory, they would have to at least win two and draw one. However, it was not to be: the students won the next two matches before the company worker's Taishō salvaged some pride with a victory. The students won 5-3.

To say that the final match on Court 1 between the police versus teachers was competitive would be somewhat of an understatement. This is, and has been, the most fiercely contested of all the matches because the one team that the police do not want to lose against is the teachers. The reason for this is because many of the competitors are each other's *sempai*, *kōhai* and *dōkyūsei* (students of the same year) from high school and university, and many of them would have competed against each other in the past. The strongest graduates of university kendo clubs often become teachers or join the police, and it seemed like old rivalries continue into this competition. It is possibly the most physical match that I have ever seen, with lots of strong *tai-atari*, and competitors being pushed out of the court or bundled over and being struck while on the ground.

The teachers started very brightly with a convincing win by two *men* strikes (to the crowd's delight), followed by a draw. The third match also looked like it was going to be a teacher's victory after a beautiful, solid, straight down the centre *men* strike, but unfortunately for the teachers, the police managed to score a *de-gote* not long before the end to even the match. The next teacher scored a *kote* to put the teachers 2-0 in the lead after four matches, much to the delight of the crowd. Then came the comeback. On their way to winning seven and drawing two of the remaining matches, the police then dropped only two *ippon*. They made this their 43rd victory out of 43 attempts.

This was a very interesting competition, full of spirit, determination and pride. If you have the chance to see it, I highly recommend it. It is held every year at the Yokohama Prefectural Budokan in February.

The Kendo Coach
SPORTS PSYCHOLOGY IN KENDO
Part 9—Aggression in Kendo: No. 4 By Blake Bennett

Following on from No. 3 of this series, this article will examine the issues of "kitae" (forging) and "shitsuke" (discipline) in the dojo, in addition to discussing group identity, the use of jōge-kankei (hierarchical relations) and the idea of kōken-chiai (friendship through kendo) in an attempt to show how the objective of polishing the mind in kendo is facilitated. Overall, the various aspects of kendo that generate motivation in the student to willingly undergo and tolerate ongoing harsh training methods will be examined.

1. Kitae and Shitsuke

Kendo training drills are typically conducted in pairs, and it is often stated that the role of the receiver (*motodachi*) is important in drawing effort from the attacker (*kitae*) (e.g. Sumi, 2006). For instance, during the particularly gruelling exercise of *kakari-geiko*, the receiver's responsibility is not only to prompt a high level of effort, but to increasingly challenge the attacker to break past their physical boundaries by pushing, blocking and denying insufficient cuts or poor technique. These commonly practised methods illustrate an example of the type of pedagogy performed with the "intent to help" through *kitae* (forging) and that aim to develop the physical, mental and spiritual qualities of the student, yet from the outside may appear to be outright bullying.

Also, the *motodachi* (receiver or training partner) may justify using the *shinai* to strike unprotected areas of the attacker's body, or doing *mukae-zuki* (a thrust to the throat as an attack is made) as a means to alert the attacker that there was an insufficient element in preparation for the strike or *zanshin*, and to encourage perseverance and concentration in the face of pain – a 'no pain, no gain' approach to instruction. In this way, and with the aforementioned objective of challenging the boundaries of the student's concentration, patience, and will-power (Sumi, 2006; see previous article), the act of a *motodachi* using the *shinai* to strike unprotected areas of the body to inflict a certain amount of discomfort on the attacker is conceivably, in most cases, meant with no malice. Thus, this behaviour may be classified as a form of "instrumental aggression". However, the extent to which a *motodachi* can and will employ this approach to instruction is not a simple matter, and may require more thought by dojo leaders in response to current societal attitudes.

This type of physical reprimanding (*kitae/taibatsu*) may also be thought of as an integral part of traditional instruction in kendo. For instance, the kendo practitioner is often encouraged to train with the theory of using a real sword in mind in order to retain a connection to the origins of kendo, and to avoid total 'sportification' of the art. Therefore, the pain of being forcefully stopped by a *motodachi*'s *shinai* through *mukae-zuki* is certainly more alarming than dying a 'virtual death' in training on the end of a pretend sword. In this way, the pain of *mukae-zuki* can in fact act as a type of 'positive punishment' by means of 'operant conditioning' (Gill et al, 2008; Skinner, 1953).[1] Although such a corporal approach to physical education is quickly meeting resistance in most areas of education and society, particularly in the West, the player norms and unwritten rules of kendo training still validate this method of instruction as a traditional part of martial culture.

Interestingly however, gradual changes in the attitudes of Japanese society in recent times concerning the extent to which *kitae* should be carried out by physical education teachers have resulted in considerable implications for teachers in school kendo dojo. Even though the belief remains in many seasoned kendo instructors that a lack of *kitae* leads to weaker spirits in the younger members of the club, many teachers are faced with making judgments as to which student is actually equipped to cope with harsh training methods. This therefore requires a firm monitoring of the dynamics between *sempai* (senior) and *kōhai* (junior) members of a club during a *kakari-geiko* session (Sakudō Masao, personal communication, 2010; Kanzaki Hiroshi, personal communication, 2010).

2. Jōge-kankei and Kōken-chiai

A general emphasis on social rank and hierarchy throughout Japanese history has resulted in a decidedly vertical orientation of Japanese society and culture (Donohue, 1991). As such, in many school kendo dojo the *jōge-kankei* system of vertical hierarchical relationships gives the older students the power and responsibility of guiding their younger club mates— passing on knowledge and the accepted customs of the dojo, ideally on the premise of *kōken-chiai* (mutual respect and friendship through training together with swords).

The *sempai* recreates personal experience and imitates the behaviours of the sensei—commonly understood in terms of the teacher and student walking the same path, and explainable in terms of the 'social learning theory' (see part 2 of this series). The belief exists that one's *sempai* has been through the trials of *kitae*, and as a result is stronger physically, technically and spiritually. In response, it is therefore deemed important for the *kōhai* to undergo a similar set of experiences in order to develop an appreciation for the values associated with hard training, and thus pass on the torch.

Importantly, Sumi (2006) states that as a result of a strict yet caring style of instruction—referring to the intent of the senior to use strict *kitae* while adopting a caring attitude that aims to 'help/teach' the junior—the student is compelled and inspired to commit fully to his attacks and overall training despite the hardship. Therefore, regardless of the outwardly aggressive appearance of certain acts of *kitae*, for instance in *kakari-geiko*, the perception that both the *motodachi* and the *kakarite* are putting their body and mind on the line for the shared goal of the development of technique and character means that a mutual respect is created and sustained. Thus, through this concept of *kōken-chiai* within kendo training, both the intent to help (rather than the intent to harm) by the *sempai*, and a positive perception of the *motodachi*'s intent by the *kōhai*, may help to explain and differentiate the forms of *kitae* from acts of *ijime* (bullying).

3. Cohesion as a Function of Harsh Training in Kendo

The rigours of training within a dojo setting can serve a number of practical functions. One such example includes the creation of a sense of shared experience and therefore solidarity between members (Donohue, 1991). This, Donohue continues, also acts to heighten any existing distinctions between members and

---

[1] 'Positive punishment' occurs when a behavior (response) is followed by a stimulus, such as introducing a shock or loud noise, resulting in a decrease in that behavior.

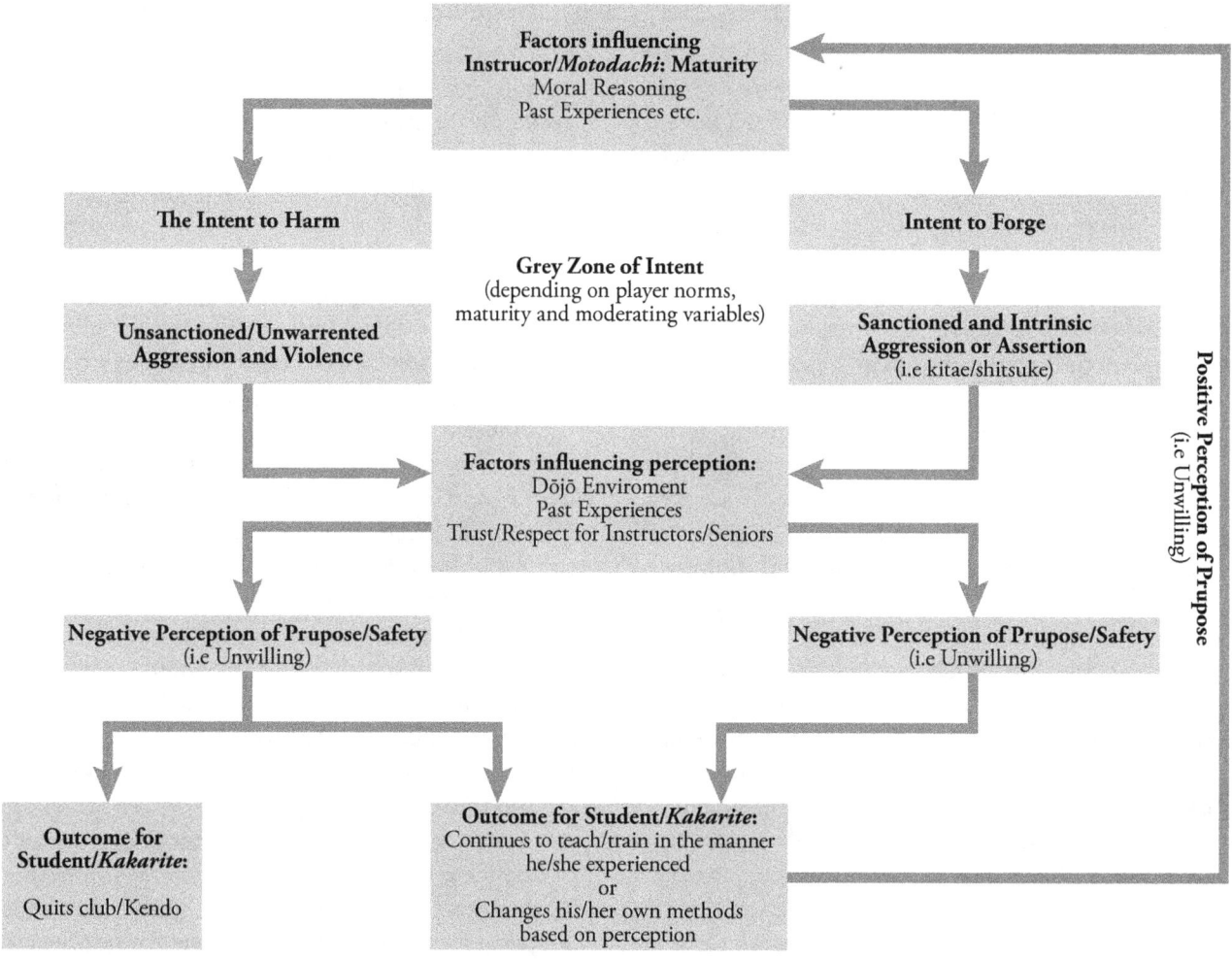

Diagram 1: The factors influencing aggression and kitae in kendo training

non-members as the assumption may exist that it is only the club members who "possess the inclination, technical knowledge, and stamina" to engage in such a harsh type of training (1991, p. 174). The extreme levels of physical exertion required by kendo practitioners therefore act to dissuade the fainthearted and insincere within the group, regardless of the exotic surroundings of the dojo, the rituals and the specific language. Budo training is simply hard work (1991, p. 174).

For those who continue, however, the achievement of such group cohesiveness as a by-product of the shared experience in everyday training, and in particular harsh training, is a goal of coaches in all sports. For instance, whether the sport or budo is an individual or team pursuit, a cohesive group identity within a club works to increase effort and the chances of reaching performance goals, and aids in the satisfaction and emotional needs of the group members (Gallucci, 2008). Additionally, and also importantly to kendo in Japan, with regards to declining birthrates, is the effect of a cohesive group on member retention (Carron, 1984). In this way, it becomes clearer how the overall desire to become and remain an accepted member of the group demonstrates why athletes adapt to the 'moral atmosphere' (Bredemeier et al, 2008; Tucker et al, 2001) of the club, and eventually adopt and transmit the group's established player norms—sometimes regardless of one's better moral judgment.

4. The Desire to Undergo Harsh Training —Positive Perceptions of Purpose and Safety

So far these articles have looked at the aggressor's intent to cause harm as a critical aspect in determining behaviour as unnecessarily aggressive. The aggressor's intent, though difficult to ascertain, helps to characterise a certain behaviour as either an intrinsic and indispensable training method, or one that crosses this fine line in kendo and is, at its core, malicious and harmful. Also, as the previous articles have shown, the objective of modern kendo training is not solely to develop the physical body, but to utilise this physical training to cultivate and strengthen the mental and spiritual aspects of one's character. Therefore, as a final addition to this discussion concerning the rationale of harsh training methods in kendo, consideration will now be given to the circumstance where 'the motive of the victim to avoid a harmful behaviour' (LeUnes and Nation, 1989; Baron, et al, 1994) is absent. In this regard, the following will suggest the possible reasoning of a student who willingly undergoes and tolerates harsh training regimens, and also the elements that allow the athlete to feel safe within this harsh environment.

It could be assumed that the victim's impulses to persevere in the face of definably aggressive treatment are explainable in terms of the physical and mental benefits they perceive will be gained from harsh training—such as those espoused by both the "Purpose of Kendo" and the "Mindset of Kendo Instruction" as defined by the All Japan Kendo Federation. However, for this 'perception of purpose' (of hard training) to be recognised as positive by the athlete, there needs to be confidence that the type of training methods they are being subjected to is warranted as a form of legitimate and controlled behaviour. That is, it is not excessive, is pitched at the correct physical and mental level of the athlete, is conducted in an organised and supportive training environment that promotes the intent to help rather than harm, and is conducted by an instructor with authentic expert power (i.e. skill) (Nakamura, 1996).

Further, this positive perception of purpose can be contrasted by a negative perception of purpose where one or more of the above factors is missing within the training environment. This type of situation creates a perception of safety, which is, as Nakamura (1996) suggests, the athlete's assessment of their own personal security during training. Largely dependent on the relationship with the instructor—that is, the level of trust and respect present within the training environment—it is thus based on the degree to which an athlete feels the instructor cares for their emotional and physical wellbeing (Nakamura, 1996).

Therefore, within this sense of safety and regardless of the actual intent of the aggressor, cases where definably aggressive teaching methods are conducted (such as the overuse/misuse of *mukae-zuki*, or hitting an opponent in unprotected areas) can be, and in many cases are perceived positively by the student either masochistically, or with the belief that one might glean greater physical, mental or spiritual benefits. This additional aspect regarding the willingness of the student to undergo aggressive training rather than avoid it is another factor for consideration when assessing the appropriateness of a behaviour during kendo training.

5. A Summary of Articles 3 & 4

Over the last two articles, a brief examination of both the "Concept and Purpose of Kendo" and the "Mindset of Kendo Instruction" revealed that the overall objective for kendo is the holistic development of the practitioner. This is to be achieved through various rigorous and correct training methods, while encouraging an attitude of respect and safety within the dojo. Therefore despite the origins of kendo as a form of combat, like many modern Japanese budo sports, it is not intended to cause harm to opponents. This affirms that the intrinsic actions of *keiko*, if performed correctly, may be deemed assertive in nature rather than aggressive or violent.

This article sought to explore the various aspects of kendo that generate a motivation in the student to willingly undergo and tolerate ongoing harsh training methods. It was concluded that the tolerance of borderline aggression is based on trust and an acceptance that the harsh pedagogical methods are an important tool in the course of one's character development. This point was referred to as perception of purpose and illustrates a further dimension in the discussion of aggression in *keiko*.

Concerning the issue of aggression within a *keiko* session, Diagram 1 provides a summary of the important discussion points. This diagram represents how various factors can alter the intention and seemingly aggressive outcomes of certain behaviour that more often than not, are justified as a form of *kitae*.

In the first instance, the variety of issues concerning a *motodachi*'s cognition, moral reasoning, and past experiences etc. (eg. moderating variables, Geen, 2001), seek to explain the initial intent of a behaviour. For instance, using the example of a *motodachi* pushing the *kakarite* around the back/neck/head with the *shinai*, the first box in Diagram 1 suggests that the *motodachi*'s socially learned experiences, ability to stay in control of emotion, and interpretation of the benefits/outcomes of their actions, set the scene for overall intent. However, the issue of assessing the true motivations of a *motodachi* is obviously difficult, and as such, there is an area referred to as a grey zone between either the intent to forge, or intent to harm, suggesting that there could be a mixture or overlap of each intent.

The middle section of Diagram 1 proposes that aspects such as the atmosphere that exists in the dojo, past experiences or socially learned behaviours, and the vital aspect of trust between teacher and student (*motodachi* and *kakarite*), all contribute to the way in which the behaviour is interpreted by the student, either positively as a form of cultivation, or negatively as an intimidating and unconstructive experience. Therefore, perceiving the behaviour positively suggests that, to some degree, the dojo environment and *motodachi-kakarite* relationship is such that the student feels comfortable. However, a negative perception of purpose—possibly as a result of an initial negative perception of safety (Nakamura, 1996)—suggests a concern that either the intent of the *motodachi* is to harm, or the overall club culture does not support a supportive learning environment.

The diagram also implies that there are various possible combinations within the dynamics of the teacher-student interaction. For instance, despite the good intentions of a *motodachi* in the course of a harsh training, the potential for the student to misconstrue these intents is always present.

The final aspect to this diagram suggests that assuming the student does not drop out of the club or kendo training altogether, the process will begin again based on personal experiences. This latter result may have the individual follow a similar line of behaviour, or alternatively, certain experiences and perceptions may prompt the individual to rethink and alter the methods he/she uses when filling a senior or teaching role.

Without a thorough appreciation for the various dynamics between *motodachi* and *kakarite*, kendo's intrinsic assertion in terms of brutal body contact as a combative pursuit risks crossing a line into the realm of the "quasi-criminal" (Smith, 1983b). In this way, Diagram 1 may be utilised as a basis to consider the elements that contribute to the issues of aggression and violence in kendo, and to assess circumstances as they arise.

The All Japan Kendo Federation has gone to great lengths over past decades to codify kendo's rules and curb excessive aggression and violence. However, unlike the rules of kendo *shiai* that are clear and strictly upheld, there are few (if any) similar written rules that guide kendo training. As such, behaviours deemed appropriate in *keiko* tend to be limited to unwritten rules, customs, norms and the beliefs of club members and instructors in each respective dojo. More often than not, during the important process of harsh training (aimed at discipline or character development), it is this vague set of principles regarding sanctioned or unsanctioned aggression that leads to overzealousness and the misuse of *shinai*. In this way, it is critical that harsh training methods promote the intent to forge. Although harsh training is considered an extremely effective means to instil the ideal values of kendo, clubs face increased societal opposition if the misuse of the *shinai* through violent actions is allowed to continue—impacting on the practice of kendo in Japan, and therefore, world-wide.

References

- Baron, R.A. and Richardson, D.R. *Human Aggression*, New York: Plenum Press, 1994
- Bredemeier, B.J. and Shields, D.L. *Moral Reasoning in the Context of Sport*, 2008 (Retrieved August 28, 2010 from http://tigger.uic.edu/~lnucci/MoralEd/articles.html)
- Carron, A.V. *Motivation: Implications for Coaching and Teaching*, London: Sports Dynamics, 1984
- Donohue, J.J. *The Forge of the Spirit: Structure, Motion, and Meaning in the Japanese Martial Tradition*, New York: Garland Publishing, Inc., 1991
- Dunn, J.G. and Dunn, J. C. "Goal Orientation, Perceptions of Aggression, and Sportspersonship" in *The Sport Psychologist vol. 13 issue 2*, pp.183-200, June 1999
- Gallucci, N.T. *Sport Psychology; Performance Enhancement, Performance Inhibition, Individuals, and Teams*, New York: Psychology Press, 2008
- Geen, R.G. *Human aggressiveness (2nd ed.)*, Milton Keynes: Open University Press, 2001
- Gill, D.L. and Williams, L. *Psychological Dynamics of Sport and Exercise (3rd ed.)*, Champaign, IL: Human Kinetics, 2008
- Hurst, C. *Armed Martial Arts of Japan: Swordsmanship and Archery*, London: Yale University Press, 1998
- Kerr, J.H. *Rethinking Aggression and Violence in Sport*, New York: Routledge, 2005
- "Killing Causes Kendo Club to Call it Quits" in *Mainichi Shimbun*, October 23, 1999. (Retrieved October 13, 2010, from http://www.accessmylibrary.com/article-1G1-56898494/killing-causes-kendō-club.html)
- LeUnes, A.D. and Nation, J.R. *Sport Psychology: An Introduction*, Chicago: Nelson-Hall Inc., 1989
- Levin, D., Smith, E., Caldwell, L. and Kimbrough, J. "Violence and High School Sports Participation" in *Pediatric Exercise Science*, 7, pp.379-388, 1995
- Nakamura, R.M. *The Power of Positive Coaching*, Sudbury, Massachusetts; Jones and Bartlett Publishers, 1996
- Skinner, B.F. *Science and Human Behavior*, Oxford: Macmillan, 1953
- Stevens, J. *The Sword of No-sword: Life of the Warrior Master Tesshū*, Boston: Shambala, 1984
- Sumi Masatake, *Hito wo Sodateru Kendō*, Tokyo, Nippon Budokan, 2006
- Tucker, L.W. and Parks, J.B. "Effects of Gender and Sport Type on Intercollegiate Athletes' Perceptions of the Legitimacy of Aggressive Behaviour in Sport" in *Sociology of Sport Journal*, 18, pp.403-413, 2001
- Yuasa Yasuhiro, *(The Body: Toward an Eastern Mind)* trans. Kasulis, T. P. and Nagatomo Shigenori, Kodansha: Tokyo, 1990

The Budapest Sakura Cup in Hungary

By Balázs Czifrik/Photos: Kristóf Nagy

This year marked the twentieth time the Budapest Főnix Kendo Club hosted the Budapest Sakura Cup. About 120 kendoka from Hungary as well as Romania, Serbia, Croatia, Slovakia, and Russia stepped onto the *shiai-jō* to test their skills.

The purpose of the Budapest Sakura Cup is twofold: first, it is one of the most important tournaments for developing young talent; and second, it creates a chance for kendoka below *shodan* to compete without limitations. The level of the competitors at the tournament was clearly demonstrated two weeks later at the 2013 European Kendo Championships in Berlin, when the Romanian junior team took silver, the Hungarian junior team bronze, and the Russian juniors also had an outstanding competition.

The significance of the Sakura Cup lies in the opportunities it offers to younger players. Competitors ranging from the ten-year-old "Kihon A" category to the junior teams primarily consisting of those in middle and high school, showed surprising ability, as invited guest Michel Guentleur (R7-dan) commented in his speech as the head judge at the end of the tournament. Although the matches were of a very high quality, it is important to point out that the event had a friendly family atmosphere.

The very first Budapest Sakura Cup was launched with great success about ten years after the establishment of Hungarian kendo. The cup was Hungary's first tournament for developing new talent. "At first, we limited the tournament to those below *shodan*," said Tibor Bárány (R7-dan), head of the Budapest Főnix Kendo and Iaido Club and director of the Sakura Cup. "But as Hungarian kendo has become stronger and ever-younger players are taking it up, new age groups were created. Presently the smallest is the "Children's A" group, where the average age is between eight and ten. In the beginning, there were only 30-40 competitors, and we never thought that by the twentieth tournament there would be three age groups just in the junior category alone, and eight in total."

Furthermore, the Budapest Sakura Cup has always tried to be as international as possible. We have invited high-level foreign guests to every competition. This year, Guentleur-sensei and Ishikubo Shinichi-sensei (6-dan) were our guests; and in previous years, Kamamoto Ryūtarō-sensei (K7-dan), Shikai-sensei (7-dan) from Los Angeles, and Fabrizio Mandia (5-dan) from Italy among others have visited the Budapest gymnasium for this competition.

We look forward to having more teams from all over Europe and the rest of the world come to compete in the years to come.

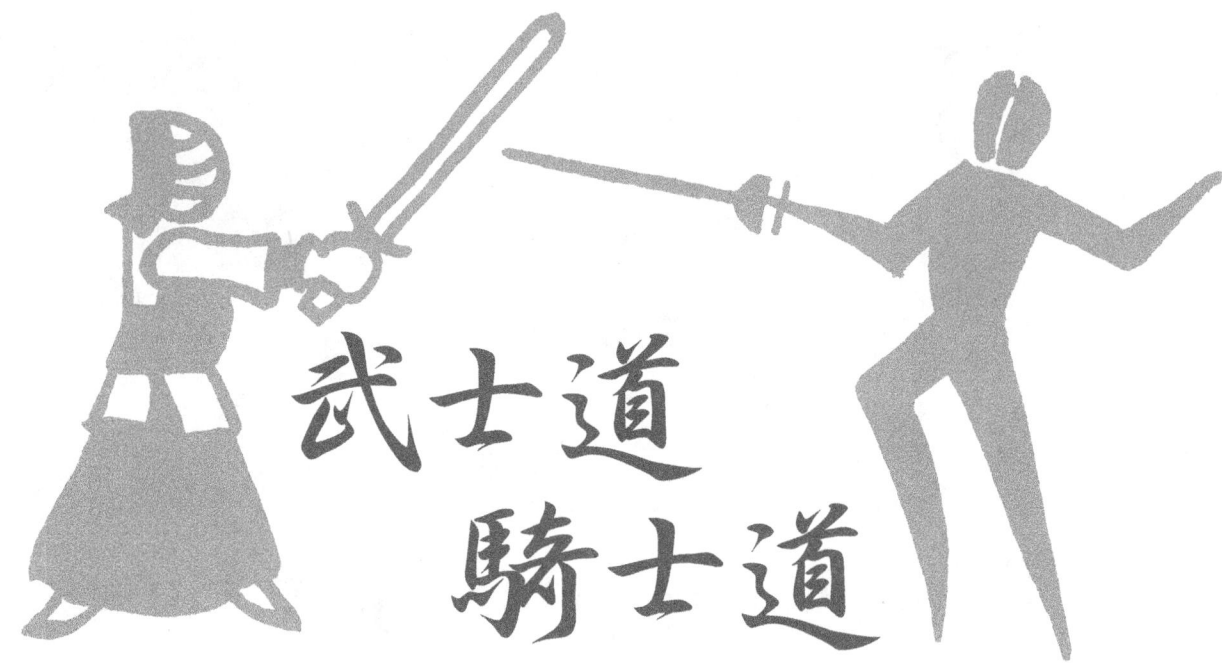

A Comparative Analysis of Bushido and Chivalry
Part One

by Ryan McIntyre

What bushido and chivalry have most in common is that they are both fraught with misconception. Emerging as geographically distant, though philosophically similar equivalents, they were not static moral codes; rather, they were, and potentially still are, multifaceted, complicated and constantly changing social phenomena. This essay, in two parts, will attempt to trace the origins of bushido and chivalry, identify and compare their core philosophies, investigate their development throughout history and discuss the influence of these two systems on both medieval and modern society.

Necessary considerations

A critical comparison of bushido and chivalry is no small task. Historical evidence concerning these two philosophies is limited and unreliable, and they have both been embellished by romanticised literature and distorted by modern media to the extent that it is difficult to distinguish historical truth from fictitious idealisation. It is uncertain from which era in Japan bushido is most observable, and is similarly undecided which European country possessed the most broadly representative form of chivalry.

Is bushido limited to the medieval warrior elite, or does it also apply to the Japanese forces of World War II?[1] While knighthood in general was quite similar across medieval Europe, chivalry varied in form and function significantly between nation, region and even individual.[2] Similarly, the polarity of public opinion surrounding events such as the celebrated 47 *rōnin* incident, demonstrate that there was no single code of ethics that was unanimously adhered to in the Tokugawa era, much less throughout all of medieval Japan.[3]

Ikegami recognises that "the way of the samurai had existed prior to the emergence of the term bushido, but it was rarely expressed consciously as a structured ideology."[4] Likewise, chivalry is understood to have emerged around the twelfth century,[5] but intellectual awareness of chivalry as a tangible code of conduct, and corresponding critical discourse

---

1 Hurst, p. 511
2 Stevenson, p. 13
3 Hurst, p. 524
4 Ikegami, p. 278
5 Saul, p. 13

did not begin to appear until a century later.[6] It is crucial to consider the fact that bushido and chivalry both evolved in accordance with significant developments in intellectual, theological, political, economic and social climates.[7] No single variety of bushido or chivalry can completely exemplify the profound cultural and philosophical development they each experienced, hence making them so difficult to compare. However, in their arguably most complete forms, both bushido and chivalry were complex combinations of martial, philosophical, aristocratic and ethical ideas that emerged during, and arguably had the most relevance in, times of civil conflict.[8]

Origins

The origins of bushido and chivalry are difficult to identify, though both emerged in a similar atmosphere of civil turmoil. In times of frequent warfare, qualities such as loyalty, courage, and martial prowess, the "vital cohesive factors"[9] of warrior groups, arose naturally in both Europe and Japan, and remained an important feature of bushido and chivalry. These early warrior codes gradually incorporated "a range of qualities which softened and civilised the conduct of war",[10] transforming them into complex amalgamations of both military and social values. In Japan, the samurai sought a common standard of behaviour to regulate their increasing power and aristocratic responsibilities,[11] whereas the catalyst for the development of chivalry was born from a progressively more sophisticated style of warfare that advocated humane treatment of defeated noble foes.[12]

The samurai first emerged in a "fully developed form"[13] around the late Heian period (mid eleventh-twelfth century) as a landed warrior elite with an agricultural economic foundation.[14] This elite class, called *bushi* (fighting man), originated from aggressive bands of eastern warriors that gained authority through military might.[15] Various social expectations, especially Confucian concepts concerned with loyalty and hierarchical relationships, as well as the deep spiritual philosophy of Buddhism that was gaining popularity among the samurai, were grafted onto this fundamental warrior code and formed the basis of bushido.[16] However, bushido, literally the "Way of the *bushi*", did not surface simultaneously with this warrior elite; rather, it was "the organic growth of decades and centuries of military career."[17]

Nitobe eloquently (though perhaps inaccurately) suggests that "[bushido] is a code unuttered and unwritten, possessing all the more powerful sanction of veritable deed, and of law written on the fleshy tablets of the heart."[18] There are in fact written accounts of bushido, though the degree to which they express the sentiments of the samurai is uncertain. While many samurai families wrote codified house laws, known as *kahō*,[19] that expressed several Confucian-influenced values central to bushido,[20] the term bushido itself, used to denote an explicit code of ethical conduct, did not in fact appear until the late Sengoku, or Warring States era (mid sixteenth-seventeenth century).[21] Furthermore, "the few Tokugawa works which worked explicitly with the term bushido turn out, in fact, to be a very narrow stream of thought essentially out of touch with the broader spectrum of Confucian ideas to which most of the samurai class adhered." [22]

Hagakure bushido, for example, seemed to condemn rationality, material attachment and "polished words"[23] in favour of swift and decisive action,[24] "the most eloquent visible presentation of [a samurai's] internal quality."[25] Perhaps this is why such little intellectual literature concerning bushido appeared until well after the establishment of the samurai and their complex behavioural code. This is not to say that the samurai were unaware of the development of such a code, (terms such as *shidō* and *budō* were relatively common),[26] but it was not until an era of prolonged peace that the warrior class, seeking justification for its continued existence, began a process of critical self-reflection.[27] In fact, the *Hagakure*, protesting against the samurai's "destiny of domestication",[28] was written in these peaceful times when such spontaneous action was already considered antiquated and having "excessive attachment to the ideals of the late sixteenth century." [29]

The origin of chivalry follows a similar pattern

---

6 Rodriguez-Velasco, p. 17
7 Saul, p. 13. Painter, p. 1
8 Stevenson, p. 3, 19. Hurst, p. 516
9 Strickland, p. 30
10 Saul, p. 12
11 Nitobe, p. 7
12 Strickland p. 30. Saul, p. 12
13 Ikegami, p. 51
14 Ibid.
15 Ibid. p. 61.

16 Nitobe, 7
17 Ibid. p. 6
18 Ibid.
19 Hurst, p. 515
20 Ibid. p. 514
21 Ibid.
22 Ibid. p. 515
23 Ikegami, p. 278
24 Hurst, p. 525
25 Ikegami, p. 278
26 Hurst, p. 515
27 Ikegami, p. 278
28 Ibid. p. 279
29 Hurst, p. 515

of social and moral protocol being combined with the martial virtues of an elite warrior class, though its development is arguably more straightforward. While bushido and chivalry both began to emerge in the twelfth century,[30] reflective literature exploring chivalry appeared comparatively much sooner than the equivalent literature on bushido. There are even well-documented accounts of explicit written guidelines defining the tenants of chivalry.[31] While this does not imply a more acute awareness of a tangible code, it does suggest a more active attempt to understand it intellectually. This is likely due to the fact that the primarily martial elements of bushido retained relevance for longer due to Japan's turbulent history, whereas Europe experienced more times of peace, and by association, opportunities to reflect on the position of the warrior in everyday society.

Some historians suggest that Christianity was the key factor in shaping the knightly warrior code. In an era when military might held more substantial influence than the law, Christianity served to temper the aggressive tendencies of warriors and cultivate ethical consciousness,[32] as well as instil discipline and morality in young, inexperienced soldiers.[33] However, Strickland warns against overstating the importance of Christianity's role in the emergence of chivalry: while Christianity indeed permeated nearly every aspect of life, and naturally came to influence the development of chivalry, "a common adherence to Christianity by no means guaranteed a uniformity of conduct in war."[34]

Warfare in Europe was formerly surprisingly savage, with mutilation, rape, execution and pillage of the defeated being commonplace.[35] In 1066, William the Conqueror defeated the Anglo-Saxons at the Battle of Hastings, using cavalry, which the Anglo-Saxons crucially did not use (as they rode to battle and dismounted).[36] Chivalry shares the same etymological roots as cavalry, both deriving from the French "chevalier", meaning horseman.[37] A knight was, in essence, a heavy mounted warrior.[38] As the decisive Norman victory of 1066 illustrates, the effectiveness of cavalry changed combat to the extent that foot soldiers were almost no longer necessary.[39]

However, the great cost in maintaining heavy armour, weapons and a war horse had a significant influence on the way wars were waged; "the emergence of cavalry encouraged the development of a social elite for one very straightforward reason: it greatly increased the cost of warfare, so that only the rich could then afford it."[40] The Normans, as a result of the advent of this new wealthy warrior class, had developed a code that advocated treating fellow nobility with respect, including defeated enemies.[41] While these ideas arose partially from steadily increasing affluence and more sophisticated social expectations, it also had practical benefits, as captured nobles could be ransomed for considerable sums of money.[42]

While bushido and chivalry emerged in similar historical contexts, it is difficult to trace an exact beginning. It is imperative to consider whether knights and samurai consciously acted out of awareness of a well-defined code of conduct, or simply adhered to a loose collection of social standards and behavioural expectations. It is perhaps not unreasonable to suggest that bushido and chivalry are no more than "a name for that general spirit or state of mind which disposes men to heroic and generous actions, and keeps them conversant with all that is beautiful and sublime in the intellectual and moral world."[43]

Ethos and ideals

As the uncertainty of their origins would suggest, defining the core philosophies of bushido and chivalry is a complicated matter. A number of historians note central elements of chivalry as bravery, honour, correct courtly conduct, gallantry, generosity, and loyalty,[44] and also the admiration, protection, and seeking the favour of women.[45] Courtesy and dignity were also considered important; Edward III is famously said to have taken French and Scottish noble prisoners hunting and seated them in places of honour at tournaments.[46]

Nitobe's description of bushido, while perhaps idealised, follows a surprisingly similar pattern: he mentions "self-control", "justice", "benevolence", "mercy", "politeness", "truthfulness", "courage" ("only exercised in the cause of Righteousness")[47] among various others. Samurai children were educated in not only a variety of martial arts, but literature, history, calligraphy and philosophy.[48]

---

30 Rodriguez-Velasco, p. 17. Ikegami, p. 51
31 Stevenson, p. 5. Milby, p. 16
32 Meller, p. 5
33 Ibid. p. 14
34 Strickland, p. 30
35 Saul, p. 12
36 Ibid.
37 Milby, p. 13
38 Ibid, p. 14
39 Strickland, p. 31

40 Saul, p. 14
41 Ibid. p. 8
42 Ibid. p. 13
43 Digby, p. 86
44 Milby, p. 14
45 Stevenson, p. 131
46 Mills, p. 10
47 Nitobe, pp. 9-31
48 Ibid. p. 29

Similarly, in England all barons and freeholders were required, by law, to send their eldest son, who would very likely become a knight, to grammar school until they had perfect Latin, where they would then proceed to study law and art.[49]

This clearly illustrates the importance of not just military prowess, but intellectual pursuits within the greater systems of bushido and chivalry. Being knighted meant being granted a title and becoming a noble; while most knights were born into the nobility, in stark contrast to the strict Confucian-based hierarchy of medieval Japanese society, in theory, anyone could become a knight.[50] In reality, however, a knight's social position was determined far more by his noble ancestry than his adherence to chivalry.[51] Similarly, in Japan, a samurai's position within the *seken*, the intricate network of relationships that comprised warrior society, was largely determined by the deeds of one's forbears.[52] Any harmful action towards a samurai's *ie*, or family, within that society was considered a grave offense. Lord Ōishi Kuranosuke, the chief instigator of the 47 *rōnin*, was arguably acting less out of revenge for his fallen lord, and more out of discontent that the Asano position within the *seken* was not fully restored by the shogunate.[53]

In addition to generic civilised qualities, religion formed a major component of both bushido and chivalry. Renowned chivalry scholar Maurice Keen describes the code as "an ethos in which martial, aristocratic and Christian elements were fused together."[54] The dynamic between the Church and the military elite of medieval Europe was an interesting one. During the crusades of the twelfth century, Christianity was especially prominent. This was largely because it fulfilled the very practical roles of providing unity among the knights (who had no central leader), granting justification for killing (in the name of God), and encouraging further acts of bravery in the soldiers (who resolutely believed they were divinely protected).[55]

While chivalry was by no means secular in nature, the zealous dedication to Christianity waned as courtly life and social reputation became more important.[56] On the other hand, Buddhism had a much more tangible and important impact on the core ethos of bushido. Buddhism "furnished a sense of calm trust in fate, a quiet submission to the inevitable, that stoic composure in sight of danger or calamity, that disdain of life and friendliness with death."[57]

Confucian notions were also intricately tied up with the beliefs of bushido, chief among which was loyalty. While loyalty was not as noticeable a factor in chivalry, likely because a knight was expected to be loyal to God before anyone else,[58] a similar focus on feudal loyalty also existed within knightly society.[59] One of a knight's principal duties was to ride to battle at the behest of his lord; however this action in itself "implied no personal merit",[60] and was in reality simply a contractual obligation in exchange for the knight's land.[61]

While there certainly would have been some unconditionally loyal samurai, the relationship between lord and vassal was almost identical to this knightly, that is, contractual form.[62] In medieval Japan, loyalty was promoted as model behaviour, and laws and edicts were issued by various *daimyō* during the Sengoku era urging against disloyalty.[63] The stress on loyalty is perhaps evidence of how widespread betrayal actually was.[64] Archer suggests that *zanshin* was a core feature of samurai culture and etiquette that has been preserved through, and is still visible in Japanese martial arts. Meaning "remaining heart" and implying a state of constant alertness, (or, as Archer suggests, distrust of one's foe), *zanshin* demonstrates that this distrust, as a result of widespread betrayal, imprinted itself onto martial philosophy and exercise.[65]

Honour was another major value within both chivalry and bushido. Nitobe presents a particularly interesting, although admittedly outdated and perhaps overestimated interpretation of samurai honour. Honour, a "vivid consciousness of personal dignity and worth",[66] went hand-in-hand with one's reputation. Nitobe suggests that "life itself was thought cheap if honour and fame could be attained therewith: hence, whenever a cause presented itself which was considered dearer than life, with utmost serenity and celerity was life laid down."[67]

In order to advance one's position within warrior society, and perhaps more importantly, to leave behind a heroic reputation after death, samurai

---

49 Stevenson, p. 19
50 Milby, p. 14
51 Stevenson, p. 9
52 Bennett, 2012/10/29
53 Ibid.
54 Stevenson, p. 3
55 Ibid. p. 12
56 Ibid.
57 Nitobe, p. 7
58 Milby, p. 16
59 Meller, p. 3
60 Ibid.
61 Ibid.
62 Hurst, p. 518
63 Archer, p. 87
64 Ibid.
65 Ibid.
66 Nitobe, p. 22
67 Ibid. p. 26

often sought to gain or protect honour even at the cost of their lives. *Seppuku*, ritual suicide through disembowelment, was closely correlated to this concept.[68] It was essentially a method in which a samurai could retain, regain or demonstrate his honour and moral purity [69] through self-willed, and self-controlled death.[70] Although the practice became gradually more structured and symbolic, it originated in situations where a warrior was faced with almost certain death, and most likely torture, at the hands of his enemy. Suicide prevented this torture and denied one's enemies the honour of killing.[71] However, *seppuku* was not actually as common an occurrence as modern media would have us believe.[72]

In contrast to this, the Christian Church did not condone killing other humans (although they did recognise the importance of the knights' ability to promote the faith during the crusades),[73] and especially condemned suicide.

Attaining personal glory was another factor, closely linked with honour, common to chivalry and bushido. Knights would seek each other out on the battlefield for individual combat, and in extreme cases, would even be more concerned with private encounters than the overall success of their army.[74] Some historians have suggested that military feats were, if not the most important, certainly the most visible aspect of early chivalric culture.[75] The notion of one-on-one combat was generally considered chivalric and honourable, though the chaotic reality of medieval warfare meant that this kind of contest was in reality only witnessed in tournaments.[76]

Samurai also sought worthy opponents on the battlefield for similar reasons; however this tendency led glory-hungry individuals to break formation. As a result, during the Sengoku era this kind of behaviour was strictly discouraged to avoid disrupting battle strategy.[77] Nitobe, discussing the important quality of bravery in regards to this, once again provides an exaggerated insight into the nature of bushido and its influence on samurai warfare:

> "Things which are serious to ordinary people, may be but play to the valiant. Hence in old warfare it was not at all rare for the parties to a conflict to exchange repartee or to begin a rhetorical contest. Combat was not solely a matter of brute force; it was, as well, an intellectual engagement."[78]

With the screams of the dying and wounded, the deafening clash of weapons and the thick stench of blood and gunpowder, it is difficult to believe that two opposing warriors would stop to compose poetry together. However, it does reveal the slightly farfetched ideal image of samurai conduct during war.

The second part of this essay will continue with a look at the development and influence of bushido and chivalry on society, and its modern-day relevance.

References:

- Archer, Joshua. "Understanding Samurai Disloyalty" in *New Voices V.2*, pp.80-102.
- Bennett, Alexander. "Medieval Warrior Culture and the Warring States Period." *Japanese Medieval History: Bushido*. Kansai University, Suita. October 8, 2012.
- Bennett, Alexander. "Chushingura-The 47 Ronin." *Japanese Medieval History: Bushido*. Kansai University, Suita. October 29, 2012.
- Bennett, Alexander. "The Ideal of 'Death' and Seppuku." *Japanese Medieval History: Bushido*. Kansai University, Suita. November 19, 2012.
- Digby, Kenelm Henry. *The Broad Stone of Honour; or, The True Sense and Practice of Chivalry: 'Godefridus.'* London: 1822. In Harvard University Library, 1989.
- Ikegami, Eiko. *The Taming of the Samurai: Honorific Individualism and the Making of Modern Japan*. Cambridge, Mass: Harvard University Press, 1995.
- Hurst III, Cameron G.. "Death, honour and Loyalty: The Bushido Ideal" in *Philosophy East and West*, V.40 No. 4 (October 1990). pp.511-527. University of Hawaii Press.
- Meller, Walter Clifford. *A Knight's Life in the Days of Chivalry*. London: T. Werner Laurie Limited, 1924. (http://brittlebooks.library.illinois.edu/scripts/Done%20with%20Dispatching/mellwa0001knilif/mellwa0001knilif.pdf)
- Milby, Gary. *The Chivalrous Man: Chivalry and the Godly Man*. Enumclaw: WinePress Publishing, 2006.
- Mills, Charles. T*he History of Chivalry: or, Knighthood and its Times*. 1825. (http://books.google.co.nz/books?id=kwRIAAAAMAAJ&printsec=frontcover&dq=chivalry+mills&hl=en&sa=X&ei=j6D0ULmaMdGRkgW29IDwBg&ved=0CC8Q6AEwAA)
- Nitobe, Inazo. *Bushido: The Soul of Japan*. 1908. Gutenberg Project eBook 2004. (http://fliiby.com/file/213604/x1auzb5f68.html)
- Painter, Sidney. *French Chivalry*. Ithaca: Cornell University Press New York, 1957.
- Rodriguez-Velasco, Jesus D.. *Order and Chivalry: Knighthood and Citizenship in Late Medieval Castile*. Eunice Rodriguez Ferguson trans. Pennsylvania: University of Philadelphia Press, 2010.
- Saul, Nigel. *Chivalry in Medieval England*. Cambridge: First Harvard University Press, 2011.
- Stevenson, Katie. *Chivalry and Knighthood in Scotland 1424-1513*. Woodbridge: The Boydell Press, 2006.
- Strickland, Matthew. *War and Chivalry: The Conduct and Perception of War in England and Normandy, 1066-1217*. Cambridge: Cambridge University Press, 1996.

---

68 Hurst, 520
69 Ibid. p. 519
70 Bennett, 2012/11/19
71 Hurst, p. 520
72 Bennett, 2012/11/19
73 Milby, p. 15
74 Stevenson, p. 26
75 Ibid. p. 6
76 Ibid. p. 34
77 Bennett, 2012/10/8.

78 Nitobe, 13.

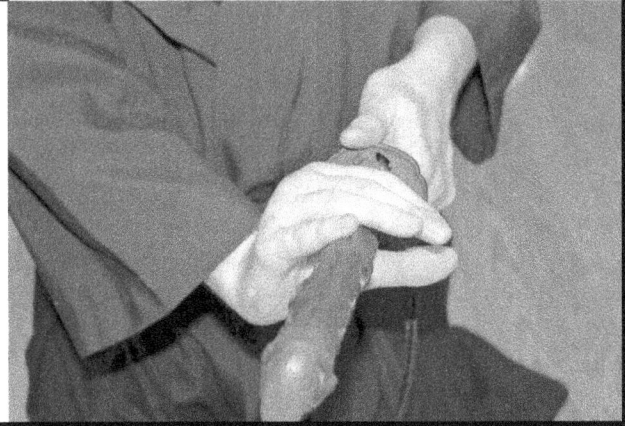

My Adventures Practicing Kendo and Iaido

By Chris Cocks

My name is Chris Cocks, I am from Regina, Saskatchewan, Canada, and I am pleased to have the opportunity to share my story with you in the pages of *Kendo World*. The story of how I ended up in my physically challenged condition is a long and complex one, so I will cover some highlights to give you an idea of my circumstances. I was born hydrocephalic, with a cyst inside my skull beside my brain. The cyst appeared to be stable and removing it would have been dangerous as my brain had formed to accommodate it. All that could be done at the time was the fourth ventricle of my brain, which was blocked, was shunted with a tube into my peritoneal cavity. I was very fortunate in that I avoided the common problems associated with this condition, including an enlarged head, mental impairment, an inability to walk, etc. For the most part I was a fairly normal child, though I never had good balance, and was never able to ride a two-wheeled bike. Other than that, I just knew that I was not very good at physical activities or sports, and when I did participate, I had to be careful of my head. Things went well, and I only had a minor problem with my shunt when I was seven years old; it had become disconnected as my body had grown.

It was some time after the surgery to fix my shunt that my parents noticed that I was developing a curve in my spine, which is called scoliosis. The specialists were not able to explain the cause of my scoliosis, but I remember hearing that the causes of most scoliosis cases are never clearly determined. So, for a number of years I had to endure wearing a variety of back braces which tried to correct the curvature. During this time I remained active and participated in the various levels of the Boy Scouts; going on hikes and the occasional camping trip.

Over the years my spinal curvature had been slowly getting worse, and when I was 14 it was decided that I needed surgery to fix my spine in place. It was also noticed that my right side was slightly, but perceptively weaker than my left, and my right hand seemed to be tightening up. At the time it was thought that this was a side effect of the cyst and malformed brain had on my normal physical development. Although my body and legs basically developed normally, the bones in my arms are not as big as they should be, and although it has never caused me any problems, my arms are skinnier than they should be, too.

1987 was a chaotic year. In March I went to the Sick Children's Hospital in Toronto to have a spinal fusion, and because of the cyst, extra-special care was needed. After a detailed examination by neurologists, it was determined that the cyst had in fact been growing slowly over the years, and had started to push its way into my spinal column, the pressure of which in turn caused the scoliosis. So, before I could have the spinal fusion, a second shunt was inserted along-side the first to drain the cyst into the peritoneal cavity. I then had most of the rest of the year to recover and build strength for the more grueling spinal surgery, which took place in December of that year.

Both surgeries were very successful, but there were some remaining affects: my spine was still a little curved, as was my rib cage; I walked with a bit of a limp because of the unevenness of my legs due to the shifting of my pelvis; and most importantly, I still had some weakness/paralysis on my right side. My right shoulder was not very flexible. Furthermore, the tissue connecting the tendons in my right hand had wasted away and now floats free, which makes my hand naturally form a claw, and it is not very flexible either. That it took so long for anyone to put all the small clues together and figure out that the cyst had entered my spine seems amazing, but my case was very asymptomatic; while the signs were there, their impact was very subtle and slow. This was also in an era before most of the medical diagnostic equipment that we take for granted today was available. When I had my first MRI scan, the technology was still new and amazing. In the end, everything worked out reasonably well.

Sorry for the long introduction, but I felt it was necessary to understand what I have experienced and what I am working with. The next 12 years saw me complete high school, graduate from university and work a couple of office jobs, which led me to working in provincial government in 1999, coordinating a Year 2000 project.

While on a business trip to Toronto I had some time to browse through a book store, much larger and with a far superior selection than I usually had available at home. It was there that I found a book on kendo. I remembered how Mark Hamill had learned some kendo while preparing for his light-saber duel in *The Empire Strikes Back*, and decided to pick it up. Martial arts like karate, judo, *etc.* were readily available, but I never thought that I would be able to take any up. Reading the kendo book showed me a different approach or way of thinking about martial arts, one that didn't have to be about getting physical in a hand-to-hand kind of way.

While I was not sure about wearing armour and participating in competitions, since I could not get struck on the head, I was particularly attracted to the different *shinai waza* and *kata*. So I set out to try to find kendo in my relatively small city. Surprisingly, it was not that hard. After asking around at one of the other martial art dojo, I got the contact information of an aikido sensei who also practised kendo.

The first night I was able to go to see a practice was the first step on the road I have been on ever since. The Regina Kendo Club was small, with only a handful of members. At the time they were practising in an elementary school gym in the evenings. The first night I went there were only two members present; a Canadian man and a Japanese man. The Japanese fellow was a university student studying for a business degree, the same as I had. He and I are friends to this day, and meet up once a year now that we are both in Japan.

The following lesson I met the sensei, Dr. Hiroaki "Rocky" Izumi. Izumi-sensei was a very unique individual: a professor of business and human resource management, and a practitioner of aikido and kendo. Throughout his career he also worked in security consultation, had been Steven Seagal's bodyguard, and a bounty hunter in Texas, among other things that sounded incredible. Rocky, as everyone called him outside of the dojo, was a fun and lively man with many interesting stories, but also a deep and serious appreciation and respect for the traditions and training in budo.

When I first met Rocky and started kendo, I was certainly mobile but very tight, and had a limited range of motion in my upper-body. My self-image and demeanour was also quiet and introverted. Through continual *suburi* practice my upper-body gained strength and, although still restricted, I developed a degree of flexibility that surprised everyone around me. Learning how to breathe from the *hara* (*fukushiki kokyū* - deep diphragmatic belly breathing) also helped me greatly in my daily life as it taught me how to breathe below the curve in my spine and rib cage. I am now rarely short of breath despite my reduced lung capacity. My legs also loosened up considerably to the point that I could sit in *seiza*, something that was not possible before.

As I had suspected, I was never able to participate in *shiai*, but I practised right along with everyone else during drills. In time, I was even put in charge of teaching the new students while the others sparred. I also served as club president and managed the equipment orders from Japan.

Though I was not able to fully realise my dreams of practising kendo, I was introduced to iaido. I would never have believed that there was a martial art still practised that used a real sword. Unfortunately, iaido is nowhere near as popular in Canada as kendo, so there was no local dojo at which to train. I found a sensei in Vancouver, Maneker-sensei, who I was able to visit on two occasions, including a four-day seminar where I began learning the All Japan Kendo Federation Seitei Iaido Kata.

Later on, another Japanese university student joined our dojo. He had already finished university in Japan and was going to be a high school English teacher, but came to Canada to study linguistics and improve his English abilities. He introduced me to the Japan Exchange and Teaching Programme (JET). As my job in government was only a temporary contract, I was free to look at new opportunities. I finally made it to Japan in September 2002 as an Assistant Language Teacher (ALT) with JET. Although I had hoped to be placed somewhere in the Kanto or Tokai regions, I ended up in a junior high school in Okinawa.

In Okinawa, karate is of course hugely popular, with dojo practically on every block. As such, I was worried that an iaido dojo would be hard to find. My Japanese supervisor knew of an aikido sensei, down the street from me, who also did "something with a sword", and introduced me to him. Ōshiro-sensei owned a little record and electronics store and taught aikido at a small dojo in his house. He also practised *battō-jutsu*, which he agreed to teach me.

After a little more searching, my supervisor also found an iaido dojo, which trained at the Okinawa Prefectural Budokan in Naha—a reasonably short distance away. There, I met Nakaima-sensei, a retired professor of German, who also speaks excellent English. The sensei and other members of the dojo were very understanding of my limitations, but also pushed me to go beyond them. As a result, after three years of practice, I successfully passed my 2-dan iaido grading.

After three years of living in Okinawa and successfully practising iaido and *battō-jutsu*, my JET contract finished and it was time to leave for my next adventure. As my Japanese friends had finally returned from Canada to Shizuoka prefecture, I decided to look for a job in Hamamatsu city. During that time I found an iaido dojo with Nakayama-sensei, but was only able to practise a handful of times because of my unfortunate work schedule.

Again, I was extremely fortunate that through a chance meeting, I was able to find my current job, which has been fulfilling and stable. I now live in Kakegawa city, between Hamamatsu and Shizuoka cities. Nakayama-sensei introduced me to Inoue-sensei, a semi-retired businessman who learned a respectable level of English from doing business abroad, and has also travelled the world demonstrating and teaching iaido and kendo. I have been practising with him for over seven years now. Inoue-sensei has been very supportive and encouraging of my quest to improve my iaido. Unfortunately, my location only allows me to train on weekends, and those practice times have not been as regular or stable as I would have wished. I train as much as I can, and hope that I am slowly improving my iaido and myself.

Since I started living in my current area I have also been studying *shodō*, Japanese calligraphy. Through this, I have gained a deeper understanding of the movement and pacing of iaido, with the smoothness of action as well as the combination of slow and fast movements found in both.

In March 2013, I participated in the 25th International Seminar of Budo Culture held at the Nippon Budokan Research Centre and the International Budo University in Katsuura, Chiba prefecture. I found it to be a wonderful opportunity to make new friends from around Japan and the world. I was also very happy to have the chance to try kyudo. It was pleasing to find that, despite my reduced range of arm movement, and the difficulty I have with my right hand, kyudo is another martial art that, with work and patience, is possible for me to do.

It has been a long road, with still more ahead of me. Even though I started my life with an uncertain future, my condition has been stable, and my health has been good for over two decades. Through starting kendo and then iaido, I have met a lot of wonderful and supportive people in the martial arts community both in Canada and Japan. It has opened doors to opportunities and adventures I could never have imagined 15 years ago. Although my progress in iaido has not been easy and has at times been frustrating beyond belief, it is the touchstone that keeps me motivated to improve myself physically, mentally and spiritually.

I would like to dedicate this article to the memory of Dr. Hiroaki "Rocky" Izumi, who passed away suddenly on March 1, 2013, doing what he loved: practising kendo. Without his support and patience, my life would not have turned out half as good as it has.

Не боги горшки обжигают
—It's not gods who bake the pots—
THE JOURNEY OF THE RUSSIAN KENDO TEAM TO THE 2013 EUROPEAN KENDO CHAMPIONSHIPS

By Evgeny Andreev (Photos by Nina Kalabina)

A Bit of History

The Russian Kendo Federation (RKF) has a history of more than 20 years. For about 15 of them, the Russian national team has participated in the European Kendo Championships (EKC) and in the World Kendo Championships (WKC). There are also many very talented kendoka in Russia: Andrey Solodovnikov and Alena Lozhkina have between them won seven fighting spirit awards at the EKC; the Russian junior team were the EKC winners in 2010, and placed third in 2011; Gennady Dubilin was the junior individual champion at the 2010 and 2011 EKC; and Andrey Kharchenko was awarded the fighting spirit prize at the 2011 EKC. Despite these achievements, neither the men nor women have ever finished in the medal places in the team competition. In fact, the best result for the men was a second place in the pool competition before losing in the first round of the knockout stages. The women have never progressed to the knockout round of the EKC.

In the past, the RKF has received support from Japan-based volunteers to help with the national team: Yoshiyama Mitsuru, the Russian national team coach for a number of years, and Michael Komoto, who assisted Yoshiyama-sensei and was then himself national team coach for a couple of years. These great people made huge efforts to develop the national team, and created a base for its future development. However, since 2009, the Russian national team has had no support from abroad, and has been managed by Boris Mishin, the Russian coach. He was the Russian team coach at the EKC in 2010 and 2011, and the WKC in 2012. Under his guidance, the junior team won the first ever EKC medals for Russia.

Beginning

In the summer of 2012, the RKF board decided to choose another person to manage the national team. It was proposed that I be made responsible for the national team's preparations and participation in the 2013 EKC in Berlin. It was a difficult decision to make, but I finally accepted as it was a great challenge. My mission was simply to manage and prepare the team to achieve better results than they had before.

I was sure that the Russian team could perform better than we had in the past. From the outset, I defined for myself the targets that I wanted to reach to accomplish this challenge. Through many years working as an engineer in heavy industry, I learned that in order to have a successful project, you have to define reasonable goals – ones that are achievable, but not too easy. If the Russian men's team won the first match of the knockout stages of the EKC, I could say that I had done a good job. I was sure that it would not be easy, but it was achievable. I remembered Christopher Yang's article "Do You Believe in Miracles" in *Kendo World 4.1* about Team USA's preparations for the WKC in Taipei. For me, the slogan was not, "One chance, one opportunity"; it was, as we say in Russia, "It's not gods who bake the pots."

Obviously it is not easy to prepare a good team, and with the possible exception of the USA, in Russia it is even more difficult than anywhere else in the world because of its size: there are seven time zones, and the flight from West to East takes more than ten hours. There are kendo clubs in many major Russian cities, but as the normal distance between the closest cities is around 1000km or more, and the cost of travel is usually very high, we are not able to ask non-professional kendoka to travel such distances. On other hand, it is impossible to have a good team without regular national team events. I also thought there were many local events that could also be used as team events. With these points in mind, I started to plan for the national team preparation circle.

Bon Voyage

First, I decided that membership to the national team should be free. Everyone who really wants to can now join the national team preparation circle. By the end of September 2012, we already had about 40 male, female and junior applicants from all over Russia.

The idea was to have at least one national team meeting every month until the EKC. However, it was clear that for most of the applicants it would be impossible to participate in every practice. In order to make it possible for them to join as many events as possible, it was decided to divide the applicants into zones: Europe-North, Europe-South and Siberia. These zones were meant to keep the travel costs for all members reasonable, and the number of members was more or less equal in each zone. It was also decided who would be responsible for leading the national team seminars in all zones.

By the end of October 2012, we had set up the national team calendar with seminars every month in different cities in each zone. It was thanks to the support of many people that we were able to hold these events. Andrey Kusurgashev took all responsibility for the Siberian zone; Vladislav Tolkishevsky organised the national team seminar in Kazan; Aleksey Magnushevsky was central to all events in Saint-Petersburg; Victor Pavlov made it possible to have seminars in Moscow; and many others also put all their energies into organising seminars for the national team. From mid-November 2012 we started the training program in all zones. On top of the national events, all members of the national team group were requested to participate in as many international events as they could.

I live in Paris, so it was difficult to manage the national team from France. However, I was able to practise with some of the best kendoka in Europe, and also with great Japanese teachers and the French national team members. I was well positioned to transmit that experience to the Russian national team.

EKC Application

By the end of December 2012, it was clear that all of our members were highly motivated. Everyone did their best at the seminars, even when the program was much tougher than usual. I felt that all of them had started to work as a team. At the same time, there were many formalities that needed to be taken care of, especially the application to the EKC. It might be a surprise to see such an unusually high participation fee, and it was even said that it was too expensive to include men, women and juniors in the delegation. Nevertheless, we sent a full delegation through minimising the costs for accommodation by not staying in the official hotel, but rather in a hostel close to the venue. We also asked Jan Ulmer, a former German national team member, if we could practise at his dojo, the Tekkeikan.

Russian kendo team at Tekkeikan dojo

Before the EKC

Fortunately, all of the administrative issues had no negative impact on the team, and they continued working well. But for me, it was getting harder. From New Year until the EKC, I had just one or two weekends free of kendo because I had to travel to Russia every month. My first visit of 2013 was on January 3 to Kazan. It was not easy because of the gruelling travel with no time to recover. Still, the energy of the members was so great, that we had intense sessions without needing or wanting to rest.

My second visit to Russia was at the end of January, two weeks before the EKC application deadline. After that seminar we had to decide who would make the cut and go to Berlin. For that reason, this seminar was the only one in which all members participated. We had participants from Kaliningrad in the West of Russia, and two boys from the Far East close to Vladivostok. They all took part in matches and *keiko*, doing their best to be selected for the national team. I could see we clearly had more potential members than places in the team.

After the seminar I asked all the seniors who were helping out for their ideas on who should be selected. I also collated statistics to get an objective idea. It was still difficult. Most members had no international experience, and to a degree, selection was based on guessing who would be able to perform well. Even with a clearly defined set of criteria, there were still some uncertainties, but we finally agreed on the delegation, and submitted our application.

Following my suggestion to participate in international events, some national team members got good results in competitions before the EKC. Alexey Magnushevsky and Alisa Dmitrieva both received bronze at the Dan Cup in Finland, and the Saint-Petersburg junior team, including national team member Kirill Kremcheev, did well at the Sakura Cup in Budapest.

Before we left for the EKC, there were still some seminars in the national team calendar, and one of them was in Saint-Petersburg, led by Mikko Salonen and Markus Frey, both 7-dan sensei from Finland. I asked them to prepare a special program for the national team. It was good to see people's efforts during the seminar, but it is even better when you can see them every month and notice their improvement. This seminar was another step for Russian national team development. Some national team members also went to Finland for the annual spring seminar, and for me, it was a good sign that those selected were not resting.

Berlin

When you have a tight schedule, you tend to focus on what you are doing rather than on what is to come. I suddenly realised that the EKC was upon us, and within a few days it would be clear if what I had done had been of any use.

The team arrived in Berlin in the afternoon of April 10. After checking in and a quick rest, we took our *bōgu* and went to the other side of Berlin to Tekkeikan dojo for our first practice. The team was very motivated – and it was a great lead up before the competition. The next day we had *keiko* at the venue in the afternoon. Again, our members did very well, and concentrated hard as I tried to get them in the right mood. We had a team briefing at the end of the day. The juniors and ladies had their first matches the following day, so they were given some advice: maintain concentration for the duration of the match. This was am important aspect that we had worked on during our preparation for the EKC.

On April 12, the competition commenced, and during the opening ceremony, I happy to see that we had one of the biggest delegations. First was the junior team competition. Our boys' team of Kim Denis, Kremcheev Kirill, Morozov Lev and Nam Valery fought against Hungary, Germany and Spain. They beat Spain, drew with Hungary and lost to Germany. Unfortunately, the results were not good enough to progress to the knockout round, but they demonstrated good kendo against skilful and experienced opponents.

The individual event started immediately after the team competition, and it looked as if our juniors finally woke up. Both Kim Denis and Nam Valery progressed to the knockout stages with beautiful *ippon*. Kirill Kremcheev had a tough pool of four people from which he got two wins and a draw – exactly the same as Valentin Chirea, a Romanian junior. They had a long decider and unfortunately Kirill lost, with his opponent passing to the knockout round, and ending up with the silver medal. However, Kirill received the fighting spirit award for his efforts. For a boy who has just turned 15, and who was making his debut at the

EKC, it was a very good result.

The other Russian boys in the knockout stages did not fare as well. Nam Valery lost in the quarter-final against the French junior Abou El Seoud, who went on to win gold. However, Kim Denis progressed to the semi-final and lost in *enchō*, also to Abou El Seoud. Both Kim and Nam come from far eastern Russia and this was their first European tournament. They performed very well, something their coach Vitaly Petrov can be proud of.

After the junior events, the women's competition started. Our ladies were not very lucky – the first match was against the French women. The only comment I gave to our women was that the French are not gods, and it may be difficult but not impossible to beat them. Dmitrieva Alisa, Rodina Karina, Druzhina Anna, Strelchenko Olga and Charkchan Ashkhen did well, and it was not clear until the fifth match who was going to win. However, Pauline Stolarz, the French captain and European champion, took two *ippon* to seal the victory for her team. After the French women we faced three Turkish women, and progressed to the knockout stages from second place in the pool. The next match was against the Serbian team, and luckily there was just three of them. Normally the Serbs are very strong, but having only three fighters made it very difficult to win against five. The Russian women won and then met Germany in the quarter-final. For this match, I replaced Dmitrieva Alisa with Kovalchuck because she was exhausted. However, it was clear that we had no chance against the German women, some of them having been European champions many times. Despite losing, to reach the quarter-final was a great success, especially as the Russian women had never made it to the EKC knockout stage before.

The next day was the men's team event. I was very happy with the performance of the women and boys, but this is the major event of the EKC, and the most important moment for me. We were drawn with Poland and Greece in the pool. The Russian team had already faced Poland a few times before, losing every time. I told the team that it would be very tough, so preparation was essential. There would be no room for error.

In the morning, the team went to the warm-up area and had a short but vigorous *keiko*. Then the men's competition started. The match against the Polish team was as hard as expected. Regrettably, it looked like we were not awake; the Polish team members were more focused and prepared. However, the match was not easy for them. Each *shiai* lasted the full five minutes, with one point deciding each one. We lost four matches by one *ippon*, and had one 0-0 draw. We had also lost the opportunity to place first in the pool, but second was still possible.

Next we faced Greece. I told the team that they had to forget about the earlier defeat, and they must be even better prepared than for the first match, as there are no easy teams at the EKC. Our guys did well, winning four *shiai* 2-0 and securing second place in the pool. As the next match against our friends from Ukraine was after lunch, I was a bit worried that we could lose our focus. This match was also difficult, but fortunately the Russian men managed to keep their concentration and win four *shiai* from five. We progressed to the second round of the knockout stage to meet Belgium.

Before the match started, I told the team that they had already done better than any Russian team before, and that the match with Belgium is the prize for them - they all have to enjoy it. It certainly was a hard match. Our team of Kharin Dmitry, Trofimov Victor, Magnushevsky Alexey, Kazakov Victor and Konstantinov Kirill did a fantastic job. Kharin and Trofimov managed to get the first *ippon* but ended up losing 2-1, and Kazakov Victor won 2-0. Unfortunately we lost and our Belgian friends passed to the next round, finally getting silver. Even though we did not win, in this match the Russian team was almost equal to Belgium. The only thing I could say to the team was, "Thank you very much, you guys were great."

On the last day of the EKC there were the men's and women's individual events. All of the team had difficult matches, but all of the debutantes scored *ippon* and won matches. However, only Charkchan Ashkhen and Konstantinov Kirill managed to proceed to the knockout round. Ashkhen then lost in the final 16 against Pfister from Germany, and Kirill lost in a very tough match against Ito from France.

C'est Fini

When the EKC finished, I was very satisfied with the Russian team's performance. The women reached the quarter-finals for the first time, and the men reached the second-round of the knockout competition, also for the first time. Also, two of our junior boys got awards—a bronze medal and a fighting spirit award. At face value, these results may not seem very impressive, but they are a definite step forward for Russia's development. This was a step made possible by everyone who put all of their energies into team preparation, organising seminars, and other team events, and of course, members of the team. I was also happy to see the fantastic results of my friends in the French team. I am sure that the Russian team will have similar results in the future.

A Swordsman's Evolution:
Comparing Miyamoto Musashi's Heidōkyō to Later Writings

By David K. Groff

In 2011, I was given the opportunity to write new translations of Miyamoto Musashi's *The Five Rings*, "Thirty-five Articles on Strategy", and "The Path Walked Alone", all written at the end of his life. In the research for those translations I encountered references to a much earlier text by Musashi entitled *Heidōkyō*, which had not yet been translated into English (although a basic outline of the contents appears in Kenji Tokitsu's *Miyamoto Musashi: His Life and Writings*), and decided to set about translating it. *Heidōkyō*, which could be translated as "Mirror on the Way of Soldiery" (or possibly Strategy), was written in 1605, when Musashi was about twenty-three years old (Uozumi), and outlines the style of swordsmanship Musashi practised and taught in those years, which at the time he called Enmei-ryū. Although still in the process of translation, comparing this text from early in Musashi's career with those written at its end give a sense of how Musashi's style of swordsmanship and his way of thinking about it changed—as well as what did not change—over the years. In the end, viewing Musashi's development as a swordsman, strategist, and teacher of those practices in retrospect gives a sense of what it means to be a lifelong budoka, and what this path still holds for us today.

One of the first things that can be noted is that even at this early stage of his career, in his early twenties, Musashi was already employing two swords at the same time. This goes against the common conception that this was a technique he developed later on in his *musha-shugyō* (itinerant warrior training), as he travelled around the country testing himself and his techniques in bouts with adherents of various other styles of swordsmanship. This is perhaps less surprising when it is noted that a list of techniques of the Tōri-ryū attributed to Musashi's (likely adoptive) father Shinmen (Miyamoto) Munisai, to which much of the terminology of the *Heidōkyō* bears a striking resemblance, also features the use of two swords, apparently in tandem (Uozumi, 295). This is one of a number of elements of Musashi's style—at least that of his early years—that he seems to have incorporated directly from Munisai's practice, others of which will be discussed later.

The most striking difference between the writing of the young Musashi and that of the older is that the earlier writing is much more focused on technical specifics, especially as they apply under particular conditions. In the *Mirror on the Way of Soldiery*, Musashi details how to hold the swords and how to position the feet depending on the distance to the opponent, the opponent's position, and one's perception of the opponent's relative ability. He also gives very specific criteria for how to discern a skilled swordsman from an unskilled one. From how to draw the swords under various circumstances to how and when swords can be thrown, the young Musashi seems intent on giving his students in the Enmei-ryū a clear how-to manual, a technical handbook for success in swordsmanship. In this sense, the *Heidōkyō* often more closely resembles a text like the first portion of the *Heihō Kadensho* of Yagyū Munenori, which goes into great detail about the execution of specific techniques. The older Musashi, on the other hand, is much broader in his advice; while he has specific instructions regarding such aspects as posture and how to move the feet in general, he avoids the kinds of very explicit directions his younger self was inclined to, such as, "facing [your opponent] directly, put your right foot slightly forward, extend your left arm towards your opponent… advancing, raise your long sword upright to an upper position." (quoted in Uozumi 279, translation mine) In fact, by the end of his life, Musashi is adamant that particular stances and positions do not really exist—they are merely conveniences for the purpose of teaching and to some extent practice, but do not reflect the actuality of combat. In *The Five Rings* Musashi outlines only five: raised, middle, lowered, right, and left, which he says are dictated by the conditions of the moment (but does not elaborate exactly how), adding later that:

> The raised position, depending on the occasion, may have the feeling of being lowered somewhat, and become a 'middle' position. The middle position, too, in accordance with principle may be moved up a little, and become a 'raised' position. The lowered position as well, from time to time, if raised a little, becomes a 'middle' position… Accordingly, there is the principle that 'positions' both exist and do not exist. (99)

The older Musashi also focuses much more on the "feeling" of a particular technique or concept, rather than the specifics of its execution. Whereas the young Musashi is more of a completist, attempting to spell out exactly what should be done in a variety of different situations, the older Musashi has become an essentialist, reducing all things to their elemental principles. Indeed, one of the hallmarks of the older Musashi's writing is his constant emphasis on these "principles", and the importance of discovering them for oneself through rigorous practice and investigation. While the young Musashi was no doubt very skilled, he had not yet realised the importance of these principles, and was still much more focused on the technical aspects of swordsmanship.

The writing of the young Musashi is also in some senses much more esoteric than that of the older. It can be seen, first of all, that early in his career as a teacher he employed the traditional system of "outer" and "inner" or "hidden" teachings; however, by the end of his life, he has abandoned this idea, saying "in general, since you are getting them to learn things that depend on the situation, there aren't any such things as 'deep' or 'entrance' [teachings]." (202) The young Musashi also employs a somewhat obscure system of nomenclature for referring to the areas of the sword blade and its surroundings which indicates the *kissaki* and approximately 5-*sun* in advance of it as the "past", the *monouchi* area as the "present", and the *ataru-tokoro* or "hitting place" as the "future". This terminology also appears in the catalogue of the Tōri-ryū (Uozumi, 295) and thus was almost certainly inherited from Munisai; Musashi seems to have abandoned it at some point, as it is never mentioned in *The Five Rings* or "Thirty-five Articles". Also gone in the later works is the frequent reference to "yin" and "yang" sword positions, which features very strongly in the *Mirror*. This Taoist-influenced approach to the study of swordsmanship also would appear to be a legacy from Munisai, and appears to have been quite prevalent during this era, as the same categorizations of sword positions can also be seen again in other writings of the time such as the Yagyū school's *Heihō Kadensho*. By the time of his later writings Musashi has dispensed with this almost entirely, preserving it only in his description of how the feet should be used: "… just as yin and yang alternate, the feet tread right-left-right-left. There shouldn't be any repeatedly stepping with the same foot." (89-90)

While over the years he may have lost much of his enthusiasm for the Taoist yin-yang framework for analysing the elements of swordsmanship, he picked up another philosophical framework: a Buddhist one. Given the frequent references to Buddhist imagery in *The Five Rings*—from a mention of bowing to Kannon in the introduction, to examples like "taking a model of 1-*shaku* and from it building a giant statue of the Buddha" (58)—as well as the great deal attention given to concepts clearly influenced by Buddhist thought, such as *munen-musō* ("no thought, no form") and especially that of *kū* or "emptiness", Buddhist references are for the most part conspicuously absent in the writing of the younger Musashi. The older Musashi is also fond of using the word "*kufū*", meaning to improve through experimentation, but whose roots are in a Buddhist expression meaning to work through a difficult philosophical proposition. The use of this expression points to one further contrast, in the types of exhortations the writer issues at these different points in his life. The younger Musashi's most common exhortations are "*ikanimo hayaku*" ("as fast as possible") and "*tenpen kanyō*" ("constantly moving/changing is essential"), and while the older Musashi would have almost certainly with the latter imperative (although he does not use that phrase in particular), he specifically disavowed the practice of trying to move fast in his later writing: "When you become skilled in this Way, you do not appear to be fast… Especially in the Way of Strategy, trying to 'go fast' is bad." (199-201)

The exhortations of the older Musashi of *The Five Rings* instead are constantly those of practice, investigation, experimentation… and more practice. "You must investigate this thoroughly", he repeatedly tells his readers. Perhaps this is due to Musashi's inevitable awareness, as an old man, that he would not be around much longer to convey all of these things to his students (and their students, and so on), and thus they would have to learn most of these lessons for the most part on their own. The Musashi of *Mirror on the Way* is a young teacher trying to establish his own "brand" and a reputation for it; the Musashi who writes *The Five Rings* is an old master attempting to establish a legacy.

Certain aspects of the younger Musashi's training, however, remain preserved at the end of his life. His approach to *metsuke* is largely unchanged, as is the technique of *kissaki-gaeshi*—turning the blade up from a lowered position and striking from underneath (although this appears in several other styles of swordsmanship at the time)—and the use of the *katsu-totsu* rhythm for striking from the undersides of the opponent's arms and then back down. The somewhat cryptic concept of *jikitsū*, or "direct transmission", also appears in both the early writing and the late, virtually unchanged, in both cases with the note that this is something that is taught orally and directly by the teacher. Later in his career, though—with significant battlefield experience under his belt, and presumably after having "realised the Way of Strategy" at around the age of 50—Musashi to a great degree left the technical specifics of swordsmanship behind as he expanded his vision of the Way to one that encompassed not just individual bouts with single opponents, but also large-scale strategy and further to an understanding of principles that could be applied to all of life: "… if you understand the Way broadly, you will find it in all things." (69)

In *The Five Rings*, Musashi writes at great length about the nature of "the Way". In theory, this is the same *dō*—way, path, road—that we invoke when we call our practice kendo or iaido, or any of the other budo. Over the course of his illustrious career, Musashi evolved from a technician to a true seeker of the Way, one who used the practice of swordsmanship and strategy to uncover deeper principles and truths about life in general. His focus moved from the technical to what one might call the "spiritual". What does Musashi's evolution over this career illustrate about the "path" that we have chosen to undertake as practitioners? He goes from the specific to the universal, from the complicated to the simplified, and from what might be called "understanding" the practice (albeit extremely well) to a sort of revelation. There are echoes of Musashi's path in the progress of most students of kendo or any other similar discipline: at first there is an emphasis on the technical aspects of the training. As we seek to assert ourselves in competition, we strive for things immediately perceived as advantages, qualities like speed and strength. However, partially due to the acknowledgement that these purely physical qualities will invariably fade with age, eventually we must mature, and go beyond these simple mechanical elements to a deeper understanding of principles, and ultimately to be able to apply what we learn in our martial practice in any and every aspect of our lives—to "find the Way in all things." And how do we achieve this? Musashi the old master is unambiguous about the nature of the undertaking—training, training, and more training:

> No matter how many adversaries you may overcome, to turn your back on your training is not in the true Way. When the fundamental principles appear in your mind, you will understand the mindset that allows you to overcome tens of opponents alone. Having achieved that, you will realise strategy on both the large and small scale.
>
> Forge yourself with a thousand days of training, and polish yourself with ten thousand days of practice. (125)

At the end of his life, when he wrote *Dokkōdō* ("The Path Walked Alone", or, alternately, "The Way of Independence/Self-Reliance"), Musashi had ceased to give any technical advice about swordsmanship at all, perhaps believing he had transmitted all he could about that art, and instead confined himself to a short list of concise instructions for how a warrior could best live a free and independent life. These axioms are simple and austere, of a Spartan sensibility: "Think little about yourself; think deeply about the world. … Have no special wishes about your home. … Along the way, have no bad feelings towards death. … Buddha and the gods are to be revered, but do not make requests of them." (240–241) His evolution complete, this is the hard-won wisdom of his years of training and battle in the quest for perfection of himself and the Way. As we bow and enter the training area and begin our own *keiko*, we should remember that we too are on the same path, and that daily it is teaching us about much more than just how to win, or even about respect and honour (though it is about that, too), but ultimately something about the deeper principles of life itself. Then, as we ourselves also evolve, we may truly understand what Shinmen Musashi says to us as he speaks to us across the centuries.

Bibliography

- Miyamoto (Shinmen) Musashi. *The Five Rings: Miyamoto Musashi's Art of Strategy.* Trans. David K. Groff. London: Watkins, 2012.
- Tokitsu, Kenji. *Miyamoto Musashi: His Life and Writings.* Boston: Shambhala. 2004.
- Uozumi, Takashi. *Miyamoto Musashi: Nippon-jin no Michi.* Tokyo: Pelican, 2002.
- Yagyū, Munenori. *Heihō Kadensho.* Ed. Ichirō Watanabe. Tokyo: Iwanami, 2003.

Jon Fitzgerald at centre-back. Courtesy of Team GB

On Being CAPTAIN

By Jon Fitzgerald

In April 2013, I was lucky enough to go to the European Kendo Championships (EKC) in Berlin, Germany. As a national team member, the EKC and World Kendo Championships (WKC) represent the peak of a kendoka's career. Berlin would be my third time at the EKC, in a competitive career spanning more than 12 years. I have also been to two WKC and numerous other smaller events around Europe. However, this EKC would be something different, and would present new and very unique challenges to me. The 2013 EKC was to be the first major event where I would not just be a competitor; I would also be the captain of my country. I had previously captained the national team at friendly events in Europe, such as the Five Nations Championship, and also at other events like the London Cup, and I had also been the captain of Tora, my home dojo in London. I had never been captain on a stage as big as this. Fortunately, I was able to have the chance to develop myself and grow into the role a little in the year leading up to the EKC. On the day, however, with those bright lights bearing down on you, and the weight of expectation on your shoulders, it feels like very little can prepare you for the task ahead.

Any competition is always more than just one day – it is a process that lasts for months, or even years. The purpose of this article is to share my experiences of this process and the EKC, and also my thoughts and feelings about my new role within the team. As a relatively new captain, I do not claim to have all the answers, but I hope that I can share the wisdom of some of my *sempai* and teachers, and for what it is worth, my own thoughts on what is both a great honour, and an equally great burden for a competitor. I also hope that the following ideas can help not only national team

Jon as Taisho at the London Cup (Photo ©Manuela Hoflehner)

competitors looking forward to the next steps of their competitive career, but also kendoka of any background at dojo level who find themselves becoming captains for their clubs at upcoming *taikai* and events.

The Build-up

When I was first approached by the management of the British Kendo Association about taking on new responsibilities within the national team, I asked an old friend for his advice. Simon Bradley was the captain of the national team for many years when I first joined as a teenager. He was a great captain, and is a brilliant person who I respect very much. I will never forget what he told me when I said that I would be taking on the captaincy at the national team camps. Simon explained to me that the most important thing for a captain, above personal results, was to get the best from your teammates. A good captain, he continued, was not just someone who could win their own matches, but someone who could get the best out of the people around him, and lift everyone else to their fullest potential. I kept this in mind and remembered the advice about how to approach training from Stuart Gibson, my current teammate and former captain. I set out to be an example and a role model as much as I could to the team during the national team training camps.

I pushed myself to make sure that everything that I did, *suburi*, *kihon*, *waza-geiko*, *ji-geiko*, or *shiai*, I did with 100% energy and commitment. Everything had to be *ippon*, and everything had to be done to the best of my ability. No slacking off or laziness, and no shortcuts. If a technique missed or did not work for whatever reason, I had to keep going and not stop until I had taken an *ippon*. Changing my mindset during practice at the national camps, and also at my home dojo, helped me to sharpen my own kendo. This was important in order to encourage and motivate the other people around me. I also had to overcome my own frustration and anger, and beat the natural urge during a match to show displeasure at a bad result. This was something that my sensei in London, Hyun Hong Cho (a former member of the Korean women's national team), helped me a great deal with.

I found now that I could not ask other people to do things that I was either unwilling or unable to do myself. Not only in terms of kendo and my own personal conduct, but also my commitment to the team. To make things even more difficult, at the beginning of this year I moved overseas for work, as many people do. However, something that I always made very clear to everyone was my commitment to come back to the national camps as much as I could on a monthly basis. Being with my teammates and showing them all how much being part of the team meant to me was very important. Already, the burdens of being a captain were becoming apparent, and we were nowhere near Berlin yet!

The EKC

Once the team arrived in Germany, I was to face a lot of new challenges and experiences. Being the captain and leading the team during the tournament was not the only change. For the first time at the EKC, I would not be fighting in the men's individuals. On a personal level, this was a disappointment, and was hard to take. However, I could not let that affect my motivation or my support for the rest of the team. I was also now having to help the manager and coach with logistics during the tournament, as well as overseeing the team during the free periods, and running the pre-event training time and warm-ups.

Knowing your teammates strengths and weaknesses, as well as your own, is very important. You will probably not have the chance to select the fighting order for a match, but you might be called upon at a meeting to offer your input, or share your opinions as a captain with your coach, manager, or sensei. As friends and *sempai* always told me, it is important to be thinking about the strategy and tactics of a match as a player, and even more so as a captain. A team *shiai* is never five individual matches in isolation. Every match and every result is interlinked regardless of the position or fighting order. In this regard, a kendo team match is like a relay race – every player is part of a chain, passing the baton on to the next person. Often as the captain, or in the Taishō position, that last person in the race is you. The team looks to you to finish that race and get the result, or when things have not gone well, to salvage some pride.

Thinking back to Simon's point, it is vital to create a positive atmosphere where everyone can perform at their best. Being a captain means you also have to be able to manage people, which requires a whole different set of skills on top of those needed for competing! Naturally, as a competitor we have to be somewhat selfish and determined, and be haughty to a certain degree. However, as a captain there is no room for selfishness or attitude. I had to learn very quickly to focus my energy as much as I could on the team, and be a channel for everyone else. Looking after everyone's physical and mental condition was crucial, and I tried

Jon with teammates at the 2013 London Cup (Photo ©Chris Seto)

to make an atmosphere that was focused, but at the same time relaxed and positive when it needed to be.

My biggest advice for someone who finds himself or herself becoming a team captain, at whatever level, is to let it amplify your natural personality. Do not try to change your behaviour or become someone else just because of a title or a role. Your friends and teammates know you already for who you are, and no doubt respect you for that. Do not try to be a drill sergeant, if that is not already who you are, or a big shot either. I have always tried to follow the examples of my *sempai* and former captains like Simon and Anthony Scott. Men who were humble and supportive, and would do anything for you. They were people who you would give everything for, not because you feared them or because you had to, but because you respected them, and you wanted to.

As for the *shiai* itself, if you are a national team member, or even if you are not, there is nothing I can say about matches. I am in no way qualified enough. You are already on your team for a reason, and you know already the hardship and training needed. All I will say is that regardless of the result, win or lose, as a captain you have to get behind the team always. Cheer your teammates, support them, motivate them, and whatever the overall result, fight to the very best of your ability. It is important to show a positive face, and

give the people around you something to be proud of. A captain does not have the luxury of being depressed, or sulking. We have to pick the team up and never show anything negative. Never quit and never give up – it does not matter what the odds are, or how difficult the task in front of you might be.

The Aftermath

It is important to set ourselves goals before we go to a competition. Sometimes we reach them, and sometimes we get close. No *shiai* is easy, and even competitors at the highest level lose. After a campaign we have to assess ourselves honestly and find positives, what worked and what did not? If something did not work, why not and how can we change it? A large part of this will be down to a team coach or a dojo sensei to develop in the weeks and months following an event. However, it is also important to keep notes and thoughts about your teammates. As a fellow competitor, you can have a different perspective on their matches, and no doubt your teammates will look to you for advice and feedback as well. This can be either at national team camps and in the dojo, or personally at a private level. Nothing says teamwork like, "Sorry mate, I wasn't watching!"

On a personal level, my goal for the EKC was for the team to take a medal and get positive results. While we did not take home a medal this year in the team competition (having lost to France in the knockout stages after coming first in our pool), we did take a bronze medal in the men's individual competition, when Andrew Fisher showed fantastic spirit and skill. We were also awarded a fighting spirit trophy for Stuart Gibson's amazing effort in the men's event, and his closely fought quarterfinal. Of the five fighters who competed in the individuals, four qualified from their pools, the fifth missing out after a close play-off. Tony Leung reached the last 16, and one of our newest members, J. Barnard, lost in the second round of the knockout stage after a 20 minute *enchō* with the eventual EKC winner, Giuseppe Gianetto of Italy. For my part, although I did not join them in the individual event, I was proud that the team was able to get results like this. I was honoured that we were able to bring a medal home to our country on the occasion that I was passed the responsibility of leading my friends. Of course, now the hard work begins. There is no break, and we are already preparing for the next EKC and the WKC after that. Just last weekend I took up the captain's role again, this time for my home dojo at the London Cup, where I was able to help the team bring a silver medal to the club.

So in closing, there is no doubt that being captain is hard work. It is demanding, has unique challenges and stresses, and requires a lot of dedication and sacrifice. However, it is also a massively rewarding experience. Not only in terms of personal honour, but also in being able to help and motivate others. I have always believed very strongly that the only thing that matters in competition is the person next to you. The greatest feeling in the world for me as a competitor is knowing that you can rely on someone else, and that they in turn can rely on you. That is something unique and special in kendo that only *shiai* can give you, and in my mind is an important reason for us to participate in competitions. The most valuable part of being a captain for me is not just the privilege or the medals, it is the fact that it made me a better kendoka and a better person.

Jon cheering on clubmate at the London Cup. (Photo ©Daniel Breuss)

Kendo That Cultivates People

by Sumi Masatake (Hanshi 8-dan)
Translated by Honda Sōtarō

Part 14
Making Use of Kendo Training

Grading examinations provide the chance for kendo practitioners to prove they are worthy of a promotion in rank; it is an indication of the quality of their skills and the effort they have put into acquiring them. Thus gradings are an important stage in each practitioner's kendo development. We do not practise our usual *keiko* under grading conditions or for promotion purposes, hence it is only natural to desire a valid and objective evaluation of our kendo skills. Grading candidates should be aware that, unlike during *shiai* where the focus is on winning, their overall kendo skills are being examined. This includes attire, posture, movement, behaviour and an understanding of the principles of *waza*. The *waza* that are performed on the day of a grading examination are acquired over a long period of hard training that we can refer to as our kendo *shugyō*; they are not fluke motions that we manage to perform by chance on the day. Since gradings are so important to each individual's development, high-graded practitioners in teaching positions have a great responsibility in preparing their students for them.

Have you correctly assessed your student's skills?

Candidates must prove to the judging panel that they are worthy of promotion by demonstrating well-rounded skills against other candidates who are usually of similar age and experience. This is quite a task and requires a great deal of preparation on the part of each candidate. However, I often find myself sitting on a grading panel watching a very incompetent candidate and wondering, "Why did this person even bother showing up?" I sometimes see candidates who are weak-willed, have bad attitudes, or those who simply have no coordination between their upper and lower bodies and hit with the *shinai* as if they were swinging an axe. Their performance at the grading is largely their teacher's fault, not so much their own. The questions are begged: Who is their teacher? What are they being taught? What kind of grading preparation did they receive? What direction has their training taken since their last grading? Each time we are promoted to a higher grade, a change in attitude or a more mature mindset is required to reach the next grade. Many practitioners may fail because they do not adjust their mental outlook after passing their current grade.

In the summer of my first year in senior high school I passed *shodan*, and I still remember how happy I was. After the announcement of results, one of the grading officials gave us some advice that had a huge impact on my future kendo training and that I was very thankful for. His words were, "Just because you've been given the rank of *shodan* doesn't mean you have *shodan* skills! From now on you have to train to be worthy of the rank! If you consistently train with this attitude you'll find yourself ready for your next grading without even realising it!" At the time I had no concrete idea about what kind of approach to *keiko* would make me worthy of the rank of *shodan*, but his words motivated me a great deal and this positive pressure made me

decide to train even harder.

The significance of obtaining a higher grade is not often explained to younger practitioners; something that can occasionally cause serious problems. When you, as a teacher, send your students to a grading examination, they should have an appropriate amount of experience and skill that has been acquired through both the quality and quantity of their training. Just because a certain number of years has passed since a student's last successful grading, this does not necessarily mean that they are ready for their next grading. *Shiai* preparation is focused exclusively on winning, but *shinsa* (grading) preparation should be thorough and meticulous. If you allow your students to attempt a grading simply because the appropriate amount of time has passed since their last grading, then you are doing them a big disservice. Your student risks losing their enthusiasm for training through grading failure, and young children might lose their motivation to continue kendo altogether, irrespective of grading results.

Grading examinations are not implemented merely for practitioners to test their skills when they feel like it. The main objective of grading examinations is to contribute to the correct transmission of kendo and to the development of examinees; it is a means of gauging the level of their *shugyō* and is a lifelong process. Each examiner who sits on a grading panel must have impeccable skills of judgement and each instructor must have a thorough understanding of kendo, but before this is possible, specific promotion criteria need to be defined for each rank to serve as common standards. When you observe your students in their regular *keiko*, you need to see them through the eyes of the grading examiner. Handing down kendo correctly to the next generation and cultivating lifelong practitioners is made possible by this ongoing process of practice and evaluation.

All practitioners should think about the significance of grading examinations as there is often too much interest shown in competition, results and winning. Even so, we should not practise kendo just for the purpose of getting higher grades either. Our attitude to training must be one of *jiri-itchi* (unity of technique and theory); this is why our *shugyō* includes written examinations on kendo theory and the study of *kata*. A practitioner who has incorporated the two separate entities of *shiai* and *shinsa* together into their training as if they were one and the same will most likely receive a lot of personal satisfaction from their training and is likely to continue training for the rest of their life.

In the tactical interplay of *shiai*, everything can rest on the actions of one moment, but during a *shinsa*, the practitioner must demonstrate all of their skills in a limited time. If a kendo instructor focuses on *shiai* too much, it tends to create a winner-loser mindset in their students and some may fall by the wayside. If an attitude of self-improvement is instilled into students, then they will likely go on to challenge for higher grades in the future as proof of their hard work. Higher graded practitioners can help avoid this split occurring amongst students.

Teaching methodology for grading preparation

The AJKF "Regulations for Dan and Shōgō Title Certificates" outlines the following requirements for *shodan* to 3-dan promotions:

(Section 3 - Article 14)
- A person who is eligible for *shodan* shall have learned *kihon* and their skills shall be satisfactory.
- A person who is eligible for 2-dan shall have developed *kihon* and their skills shall be competent.
- A person who is eligible for 3-dan shall have refined *kihon* and their skills shall be excellent.

The common requirements for *shodan* to 3-*dan* promotion state that the candidate must:

1) be correctly attired and demonstrate correct *reihō*
2) have appropriate posture
3) strike correctly using proper *kihon*
4) show a fullness of spirit

It is clear that assessing the candidate's acquisition of *kihon* is the main task in *shodan* to 3-dan gradings as these ranks are the beginning of the practitioner's *shugyō*. The words 'learn', 'develop' and 'refine' in the aforementioned requirements indicate that the practitioner's skills are expected to have matured over the years. This begs the question: exactly what is 'maturity' in terms of *kihon*? H10-dan Mochida Moriji made the well-known statement: "It took me fifty years to master the basics of kendo." With this insight, obviously there are many facets of *kihon* that can only be acquired with extended periods of practice and study.

Generally, *kihon* refers to all the components that come together in the production of a *waza*, and so *kihon* basically means striking techniques. However the techniques of striking lead on to form the foundations of the skills necessary to create openings or take advantage of your opponent's actions in *tachiai*. In a broader sense however, movements such as *kamae*, footwork, and *suburi*, and etiquette such as *reihō*, are also regarded as basic skills. I would suggest that you think of kendo basics as having three stages: (i) *kiso* (fundamentals) - aspects that you can train yourself to perform such as body actions and *shinai* control; (ii) *kihon* (basics) - actions and motions that enable you to strike or move in relation to another person; and finally, (iii) *waza* (techniques) - the result and interplay of applying the *kiso* and *kihon* in an encounter against an opponent. By reflecting on the aforementioned requirements, an examiner can make a judgement as to whether a candidate is making strikes with correct posture and spirit.

With this broader definition of *kihon*, I have devised the following list of basic points for instructing prospective grading candidates.

1) Striking that initiates from a natural and relaxed *kamae* without excessively raising your hips. Using correct *fumikomi* and maintaining good posture throughout the strike.
2) Giving a sharp shout produced by strong exhalation and maintaining energy in your lower belly.
3) Swinging the *shinai* up and down smoothly in one motion with either a large or small action.
4) Accurately striking the opponent's target areas with the *monouchi* section of your *shinai* (this requires appropriate judgement of distance and the ability to adjust your *fumikomi* stride length).
5) Coordination between your *shinai* control and footwork.
6) Reacting appropriately in the follow-up to a strike by either moving back after *tai-atari* or moving forward and through with *okuri-ashi*, and pivoting around to face your opponent again.

Kirikaeshi and *uchikomi-geiko* are the most effective exercises for beginner practitioners to develop these skills, but I fear that these exercises are being overlooked recently in favour of *gokaku-geiko* and *shiai-geiko*.

These days many young people are motivated to take up martial arts or sports because they are drawn to competition, and kendo is no exception. With this trend we often find that rules, etiquette, and practice of basics are neglected while more time is spent on competition-related training. Students who are pushed into win-or-lose competitive kendo by their instructors too early in their training often simply alternate between 'delight' when they or their team wins and 'dismay' when they lose. This is a pity as it is not a mindset that is conducive to lifelong development.

If a practitioner is to further mature their skills, then simply examining their kendo based on whether they won or lost in *shiai* will be insufficient: they must consider the entire content of their *tachiai* or *shiai*. If a competitor shows bored indifference, uses sloppy techniques, or just gets a kick out of competing, then they may gradually lose their motivation to practise and their interest may shift to other activities. Many of these situations stem from the competitor harbouring the notion that 'winning is everything'. This attitude seems to be taking a strong hold in kendo recently and it should be corrected.

When teaching practitioners from *shodan* to 3-dan, instructors should keep in mind that one of their main tasks is to make students aware of why they are practising. Instructors and students must both enjoy the process of teaching and learning and make results in competition a second priority to developing solid basics. Even so, developing one's skills to pass grades should not be the main objective of one's training either. If you set yourself the goal of obtaining a certain rank and you are successful, then what do you aim for next? You must have greater goals or purposes in your training than merely obtaining ranks. The first thing a practitioner can do after achieving a new rank is to act and train to be worthy of the promotion and not behave in a manner inappropriate for someone of that level. Dignity, pride and honour are important in being a dan-holder, but being arrogant or pursing notoriety through rank promotion is inappropriate. Teachers must set standards for students so that they will act in a manner appropriate for their grades. The cultivation of honour should be a fundamental teaching task for instructors even when teaching beginners.

Thus far in this instalment I have described the role grading examinations play and outlined tasks for instructors who are preparing their students for gradings. In addition to this, I will add some further points for consideration. I suggest that the judging criteria for *shodan* to 3-dan gradings be even more meticulously refined and that *kihon* play a large role in normal *keiko*. I also suggest that the focus on *gokaku-geiko* in gradings be shifted towards *kirikaeshi* and *uchikomi-geiko* so that examiners can judge a candidate's *kihon* ability with a standard point of comparison. I would also suggest that a list of the aforementioned six criteria, showing which elements were performed to a satisfactory level and which were not, could be used to give feedback on each candidate's performance. Grading examinees would then be able to take these feedback sheets away with them for further reference. I worry that over-concern with *gokaku-geiko* means that a candidate might be able to strike their opponent's target-areas through their speed or athletic ability, but that their actual strikes may be sloppy or their posture bad. Preoccupation with attack and defence often draws attention away from correct form. I also suggest that higher grades, 6-dan or 7-dan practitioners, act as *motodachi* in gradings to give candidates the best possible chance to show their basic skills, as higher grades have a better understanding of distancing and timing. I feel that this is better than having candidates of similar skill level simply attacking each other in *tachi-ai* to demonstrate basic techniques.

During the *kata* portion of grading examinations, I suggest that high-graded practitioners once again take the leading role by serving as *uchidachi* (attacker) and allowing the *shodan* to 3-dan candidates to concentrate entirely on the role of *shidachi* (counter-attacker). If grading candidates are only required to perform the role of *shidachi*, then they will be able to demonstrate their grasp of distancing, *sen-sen-no-sen* timing, *tō-hō* (sword usage) and body movements, which are the main goals of *kata*. If beginner practitioners are made to learn both *shidachi* and *uchidachi* roles, then just remembering all of the movements proves to be quite a task and the objectives and theory behind practising *kata* in the first place tend to be overlooked.

It is my hope that regional kendo organisations will seriously look into improving the standards of grading examinations and the teaching methodology of normal *keiko*.

Instructing practitioners to use kisei (spirit) and tanryoku (strength of mind) rather than just relying on their athletic abilities

In the beginning or 'introductory' stage (*shodan* to 3-dan), *keiko* consists of practising *kihon* under the supervision of a teacher and, because the process is largely physical, the content is fairly easy to grasp. However, at the 'intermediate' stage (4-dan to 5-dan), *keiko* includes more advanced elements and the main objective is to further develop *kihon* in relation to one's opponent, and therefore practitioners run the risk of picking up bad habits if they attempt to navigate this stage without supervision. Often at this point in a practitioner's life they may be focusing on their work or social activities and, even though they no longer have the advantage of the systematic training they had in their school years, more independence in training is still necessary. However, as this intermediate stage is vital in their preparation for more senior levels, they need appropriate support in balancing their life inside and outside the dojo. Generally a practitioner may be in their late twenties or early thirties at this stage and their physical development may have reached its peak.

For example, in the competitor line-up for the All Japan Kendo Championship for a particular year, the average grade of the 64 competitors is 5.2-dan and the average age is 29.6 years old. Practitioners of this age and rank will have a strong influence in how kendo is handed down to the next generation, so further guidance will not go astray. Observing the matches of these competitors and listening to their pre- and post-competition comments often gives us an indication that they are in the transition period from the intermediate stage to the advanced stage. They often mention the mental elements of kendo in their comments. The following summarises the challenges of competition as commented on by competitors.

- enduring the mental pressure of *taikai* participation
- attempting to overwhelm an opponent's *ki* with their own
- eliminating hesitation that occurs during moments of attack and defence
- maintaining concentration throughout each *tachi-ai*
- overcoming doubts that surface when observing another competitor
- maintaining the commitment to not waver during a *sutemi* attack
- overcoming impatience caused by an urge to win

These internal conflicts exist in each competitor, and they are related to skills such as judging striking opportunities, committing to fully completing *waza* rather than hesitating and only making half-hearted attempts, and judging *maai* distance. Naturally they can have a significant affect on the outcome of a match and should be dealt with in regular *keiko*. Accordingly, instructional content for practitioners at the intermediate stage should differ greatly from what they received during their introductory stage. Practitioners perform skills differently in tense situations than when they are calm, so in order to overcome an opponent, practitioners must train to perform well under pressure by controlling, withholding or releasing their *ki* as required. These mental skills are more readily cultivated through *keiko* than by reading books and listening to the advice of seniors. To help practitioners at this intermediate stage improve, the higher graded practitioners who serve as their *motodachi* should examine their own role as teachers.

Overwhelming the kakarite with kisei and tanryoku

A practitioner may come up against opponents who have a wide repertoire of techniques, have fast *shinai* handling enabling them to strike quickly, have the leg strength to enter *uchima* quickly, or have strong *taiatari*. It is the responsibility of the *motodachi* to teach the *kakarite* the importance of applying and responding to *kisei* pressure in order to deal with this wide variety of opponents. The *motodachi* demonstrates this skill by applying strong pressure on the *kakarite* and trying to control the exchange. It is important to develop *kamae* (both physically and mentally) to seem formidable even at the *tōma* distance. If the *motodachi* simply steps into the *kakarite*'s attack to perform a *debana-waza* without physically or mentally pressuring the *kakarite*,

that *motodachi* will probably be disliked and avoided by lower grades. You, as the *motodachi*, should try to face the *kakarite* at *tōma* distance and gradually close in forcing them to overcome the pressure you are applying to them; the nonverbal threat being that if they do not, they will be attacked. Ideally you should try to overwhelm them with your presence and spirit (*kigurai*) rather than by actually striking them. You should also encourage them to make straight *sutemi* attacks despite the strong pressure you are placing on them. The *motodachi* should not be lazy; you need to work harder than the lower grade *kakarite*. This enables the *kakarite* to benefit from true *kakari-no-keiko*.

Striking a lower grade kakarite who hesitated or showed insufficient seme

As the *motodachi*, you must observe the *kakarite*'s reaction to your mental and physical pressure from the *tōma* distance and, if the *kakarite* does not move or hesitates momentarily, you should close in and attack them sharply with a *shikake-waza* and a spirit of *sutemi*. This is to make the *kakarite* aware that they were in the vulnerable state of *kyo*, which means they stopped for no reason, hesitated, were mentally preoccupied with something, or had a lapse in concentration. A quick or agile lower-grade *kakarite* may manage to block or avoid this attack from the *motodachi*, but the fact remains that they momentarily exposed themselves in a state of *kyo*.

The *motodachi* should not relax their *ki* throughout the *keiko* as the *kakarite* needs to understand that they have not succeeded if they have allowed the *motodachi* to pressure them and attack them first. If the *kakarite* retaliates against the *motodachi*'s strike while off balance and under pressure, then they are not the victor in that encounter. The *motodachi* should not acknowledge or praise an attack made by the *kakarite* if it was merely a counterattack made after being overwhelmed. This is not the true spirit of kendo and it sets a bad example.

Maintaining composure when a lower-grade kakarite manages to strike you

Practitioners at the intermediate stage might often find their way through the *motodachi*'s *kamae* and strike successfully if they are physically strong or have quick reflexes. You, as the *motodachi*, need to keep your *shinai* on the centreline and direct your *kensen* at the *kakarite*'s throat and, if the *kakarite* inadvertently leaves themselves open at this moment, you must attack them to show their mistake.

I remember training under Yoshitomi Arata-sensei

who would not let up physical and mental pressure on a *kakarite* until they had made a completely valid strike. Even when I managed to strike him, I knew the strike was not valid unless he acknowledged that my spirit had overpowered him. Thanks to this kind of *keiko* I was able to execute large *men* strikes with a spirit of *sutemi* that overcame my opponent's *kensen*. With influence from Yoshitomi-sensei, I formed a habit of reflecting upon my *shiai* performance by first assessing my mindset and mental composure, and then by looking at my strikes and form. He showed me that we risk losing if our *ki* is disturbed. This *keiko* also led me to react differently when struck by an opponent; instead of pulling back I would take half a step forward with a spirit of *sutemi*. This way I was able to assess my opponent's movements more clearly because I was in a better position to counterattack if necessary. It taught me to maintain composure even when struck.

Allowing lower-graded practitioners the chance to gain a sense of the purposes of kendo training through keiko

For most practitioners at the intermediate level, work occupies a large part of their lives and finding time to train can often prove difficult. In this kind of situation they will not improve if they simply seek to hit each other for the sake of striking or winning; on the contrary, they may lose interest in kendo and quit. Practitioners at this stage must try to cultivate their *kisei* and *tanryoku*. In every training session they must make the best *seme* against their partners that they can with their *kisei* and *tanryoku* and they must strike with a spirit of *sutemi*. If they perform *keiko* like this after a day of work, they will be vitalised for the next day. This kind of training is a chance for senior grade practitioners to train their minds while bringing out the full spirit of practitioners still at the intermediate stage.

In the spiritual culture of kendo, practitioners mutually improve by cultivating their *kisei* and *tanryoku* against each other, not by besting each other with cunning techniques. The aim is to challenge one another mentally but an attitude of fairness is important because overwhelming a partner with *kisei* only is quite difficult regardless of skill or experience. Even a higher grade practitioner may be overwhelmed and struck by a lower-grade practitioner. When this happens the higher-grade practitioner should be modest and acknowledge the strike even if it was not very powerful or even if only the tip of the *shinai* made contact. Acknowledging every strike is not appropriate either. An unreasonable strike should not be acknowledged just because it landed on a target area; neither party benefits from approval that is too readily given. If you are consistent in your judgements, the lower graded practitioner will be grateful for your guidance but, if you perform *mukae-zuki* or strike back in a nasty manner against invalid techniques, you may be resented. You will not have this problem if your attitude is resolute and honest.

In my late twenties and early thirties (that being the period when I could physically strike a great deal but the number of my valid strikes was low), Yoshitomi-sensei kept telling me that I was not overwhelming him mentally when striking. I remember feeling angry at the time because I was confident that I had made valid strikes against him sometimes. Looking back now, I feel ashamed of my poor attitude. There were a few occasions, however, when he would acknowledge a successful strike of mine and also acknowledge that I had overpowered him mentally. Curiously these were occasions when I felt rooted to the spot and could not make strikes as freely as normal.

I had another teacher whose *kisei* was very strong. He kept his *kensen* at my throat, dodged or counterattacked me and I could barely even touch him. One day he asked me for *ippon-shōbu* when I was out of breath, as he often did. In the following moments I regained my composure at the *tōma* distance, focused power into my lower belly, reacted instinctively when he closed in and I managed to strike his *men* cleanly. I remember the surprised reaction of the people in line behind me, and the sensei went down into *sonkyo* immediately after this to acknowledge my winning point. I remember the feeling in my body at the time but I have not been able to recreate it since.

Kendo aims to cultivate the character, but it does not encapsulate all aspects of our being. Hard training provides us with a means to control things such as our frame of mind, determination, attitude and sense of fairness. We should try not to logically connect kendo with everything in our character—things such as intelligence, ethics or culture. I do believe however that developing ourselves through *keiko* provides a strong foundation for broadening our human nature.

In closing, I believe that practitioners must make a habit of cultivating and developing their *kisei* and *tanryoku* if they wish to accomplish the goals of kendo training. If you find yourself in charge of intermediate-stage practitioners then simply finding amusement in competitively striking one another is an inappropriate approach to training. Practitioners at this stage must be serious about developing their *kisei* and *tanryoku* against each other. In these situations higher-grade practitioners who act as *motodachi* should control how their attitudes and characters come out in their *waza* and let lower-grade practitioners realise what they need to work on by leading with physical examples in *keiko* rather than by explaining things to them verbally.

Living with Shikai

Generalised Anxiety Disorder in Kendo

by Thomas Sluyter

To retain *heijōshin* (an even mind) is one of the greater goals in kendo.

> "*Heijoshin* reflects a calm state of mind, despite disturbing changes around you. It is the state of mind one has to strive for, in contrast to *shikai*, or the 4 states of mind to avoid: 1. *kyo* (surprise, wonder); 2. *ku* (fear); 3. *gi* (doubt); 4. *waku* (confusion, perplexity)." (Buyens, 2012)

In this article, I would like to introduce Generalised Anxiety Disorder (GAD). For sufferers of GAD, every day is filled with two of the four *shikai*: fear and doubt. While I am only a layman, I hope that my personal experiences will be of use to those dealing with anxiety disorders in the dojo. I will start by explaining the medical background of GAD, followed by my personal experiences, and then finish by providing suggestions to students and teachers dealing with anxiety in the dojo.

Anxiety Disorders: Definition and Treatment

All of us are familiar with anxiety and fear as they are basic functions of the human body. You are startled by a loud noise, you jump away from a snapping dog, and you feel the pressure exuded by your opponent in *shiai*. They prepare your body for what is called the "fight or flight" reaction: either you run for your life, or you stand your ground and fight tooth and nail. However, these instincts become problematic if they emerge without any reasonable stimulus. The most well-known type of such disorders are phobias, which are suggested to occur in up to 25% of the adult US population. (Rowney et al, 2012)

With regards to GAD, perhaps the easiest ways to describe it is to use an analogy: GAD is to worry as depression is to "feeling down". Just like a depressed person cannot "simply get over it" and is debilitated in their daily life, a person with GAD lives with constant worry.

The criteria for determining that someone has GAD is that the person has trouble controlling worries and is anxious about a variety of events, more than 50% of the time, for a duration of at least six months.

These worries must not be tied to a specific anxiety or phobia and must not be tied to substance abuse. The person exhibits at least three of the following symptoms: restlessness, exhaustion, difficulty concentrating, irritability, muscle tension and sleep disturbance.[1]

Thus the symptoms differ per person, as does the potency of an episode. In severe cases of GAD, episodes will result in what is known as a panic attack, which you could describe as a ten-minute bout of super-fear. Effects of a panic attack may include palpitations, cold sweat, spasms and cramps, dizziness, confusion, aggressiveness and hyperventilation. Because of these effects, people having a panic attack may think they are having a heart attack or that they are going plain crazy.

An important element of GAD is the vicious cycle or snowball effect. As my therapy workbook describes it, a sense of anxiety will lead to physical and mental expressions, which in turn will lead to anxious thinking. People with GAD will often fear the effects of anxiety, like fainting or throwing up. These anxious thoughts will create new anxiety, which may worsen the experienced effects, which in turn will feed more anxious thoughts. And so on. Thus, even the smallest worry could start an episode of anxiety, like a snowball rolling down a slope. What may get started with *"The fish I had for lunch tasted a bit off"* may end up with, *"Oh no, I'm having a heart attack!"* This vicious cycle feeds off of assumptions, worries and thoughts that get strung together.

The treatment of GAD occurs in different ways, and is often combined:

> Medical treatment of pre-existing physical ailments or other disorders
> Medicinal treatment of the anxiety, with, for example, Prozac, Zoloft, Valium or Ativan
> Psychotherapy
> Support structures through the education of family and friends

All sources agree that having proper support structures is imperative for those suffering from any kind of anxiety disorder. Knowing that people understand what you are going through provides a base level of confidence, a foothold if you will. Knowing that these people will be able to catch you if you fall is a big comfort, and having someone to help you dispel illogical and runaway worries is invaluable.

---

1 According to the DSM-IV-TR (Diagnostic and Statistical Manual of Mental Disorders, 4th edition, text revision), a document published by the American Psychiatric Association that attempts to standardize the documentation and classification of mental disorders, and Rowney et al, 2010.

My Personal Experiences with GAD

I am lucky in that I suffer from mild GAD, and that I have only experienced less than 15 panic attacks in my life. Where others are harrowed by constant anxiety, I only have trouble in certain situations. I was never diagnosed as such, but in retrospect I have had GAD since my early childhood. At the time, the various symptoms were classified as "school sickness", irritable bowel syndrome and work-related stress. It was only during a holiday abroad in 2010 that I realised something bigger was at hand, because I had a huge panic attack. I was extremely agitated, could not form a coherent line of thought and was very argumentative. My conclusion at the time was that "I am going crazy here, that has to be it. I really don't want this, I need a pill to take this away right now!" Oddly, I discounted the whole thing when we arrived home. It then took a second, big panic attack for me to accept that I needed to talk to a professional. It did not take my doctor long to refer me to a therapist for cognitive behaviour therapy (CBT).

CBT is one of many forms of therapy applicable to anxiety disorders and it is often cited as the most effective. It is suggested that CBT achieves "a 78% response rate in panic disorder patients who have committed to 12 to 15 weeks of therapy." (Rowney et al, 2012). In my personal opinion, CBT is successful because it is based on empowerment—the patient is educated about his disorder, showing him that it does not have actual power over him and how he can deal with it. As part of therapy, one learns to recognise the patterns that are involved in the disorder and how to pause or halt these cycles. Patients are given tools to prevent episodes, or to relax during an attack. CBT also relies upon the notion of 'exposure' wherein the patient is continuously challenged to overstep his own boundaries. The senses of self-worth and of confidence are improved by realising that your world is not as small as you let your fears make it.

I have learned that the best way to deal with a runaway snowball of thoughts is to dispel the thoughts the moment they occur. Anxious thoughts often start out small and then spiral into nonsensical and unreasonable worries. By tackling each question when it comes, I maintain a feeling of control. Having someone with me to talk over all these worries is very useful, because they are an objective party: they can answer my questions from a grounded perspective. My wife has proven to be indispensable, simply by talking me down from the nonsense in my head.

I first started kendo in January 2011, half a year before I started CBT. In the week leading up to class, I devoured online resources so I would not make a fool of myself in the dojo. In my mind, I had the image that

I would be under constant scrutiny as the new guy. I feared that any misstep would make my integration into the group a lot harder. I read up on basic class structures, on etiquette, on basic terminology, and I even did my best to learn a few Japanese phrases in order to thank the sensei for his hospitality. Even before taking a single class I already had a mental image of kendo as very strict, disciplined and unforgiving, and I was making assumptions and having worries left and right.

I have now practised kendo for a little over two years, and I have found that it is a great tool in conquering my anxiety disorder in the following ways:

1. I experience kendo as a physically tough activity. Seeing myself break through my limitations forces me to reassess what I am and am not capable of.
2. The discipline in class feels like a solid wall holding me up and there is a sense of camaraderie. My *sempai* and sensei will not let me fail and I have a responsibility towards them to tough it out.
3. Reading and learning about kendo provides me with confidence that I may one day grow into a *sempai* role.
4. In kendo one aims for *kigurai*. As Geoff Salmon-sensei wrote:
   "*Kigurai* can mean confidence, grace, the ability to dominate your opponent through strength of character. *Kigurai* can also be seen as fearlessness or a high level of internal energy. What it is not, is posturing, self-congratulating or show-boating." (Salmon, 2009)
   Thus *kigurai* is a very empowering concept!
5. Kendo is such an engaging activity that it grabs my full attention. Once we have started I no longer have time to worry about anything outside of the dojo. Or as one *sempai* says, "At tournaments I'm panicking all the way to the *shiai-jō*; but once *shiai* starts I'm in the zone."

In the dojo I may forget about the outside world, but there are many reasons for anxiety in the training hall as well. For example, after a particularly heavy practice I will feel nauseous and light-headed, which has led to fears of fainting and hyperventilation. I have also worried about my sensei's expectations regarding my performance and attendance at tournaments: What if I can't attend? What will he say? Will he reproach me? Will he think less of me?

I have also felt anxious about training at our dojo's main hall, simply because the other kendoka's level is so much higher than mine. I felt that I was imposing on them, that I was burdening them with my bad kendo and that I was making a fool of myself. I finally broke through this by exposure: by attending a national level training and sparring with 7-dan teachers I learned that a huge difference in skill levels is nothing to be ashamed of. All of a sudden I felt equal to my *sempai*, not as a kendoka but as a human being.

Another great example of exposure was a little trick pulled by the sensei of our main dojo who is aware of my GAD. He had noticed that I allow myself to bow out early if I start to get anxious. So what does he do? We started class doing *mawari-geiko* (practice where the whole group rotates to switch partners), and right before it is my turn to move to the *kakarite* side, he freezes the group's rotation so that I am stuck in a position where I have responsibility towards my *sempai*, because without me in this spot, the opposing *kakarite* would need to skip a round of practice. On the one hand, I was starting to get anxious from physical exhaustion, but on the other, I would not allow myself to stop because of this sense of responsibility. His trick worked and I pulled through with stronger confidence.

In the dojo I regularly use two of the tools taught to me during CBT (Boeijin, 2007):

1. Breathing exercises: they let me catch my breath and force me to focus my thoughts on one thing. You breathe in to the count of four, hold it for two counts, and then breathe out to the count of five. Hold to the count of two and repeat. This exercise is also often used with hyperventilation issues. Various sources, including Paul Budden (2007), suggest breathing through the nose instead of the mouth, to prevent over-breathing.

2. Relaxation exercises: I scan my whole body for tense muscles in order to release them. For different sections of your body you will tighten up all the muscles for a few seconds and then release them, which is repeated three times. You start with the facial muscles, making a scrunched-up face and releasing it. Then the muscles in the neck. Then the left arm, followed by other body parts. When moving to a new part, the previously exercised one should remain relaxed and in the end you should end up with a completely relaxed body. This exercise is best done while sitting on a chair or bench.

GAD in the Dojo: For Teachers

If one of your students approaches you about their anxiety disorder, please take them seriously. As explained above, we all feel fear and have doubts, but an actual disorder is another thing entirely. You will not be expected to be their therapist or their caretaker—all they need is your support. Simply knowing that you are supporting them is a tremendous help.

In *Kendo World 5.2*, Ben Sheppard discussed the concept of "duty of care" in his article "Teaching Kendo to Children." (Sheppard, 2010). While the legal aspects of the article pertain to minors in certain countries, the general concept can be applied to any student who may require special care. It would be prudent to keep a file containing relevant medical and emergency information. This should not be a medical file by any means, but having a list of known risks as well as emergency contact information would be a good idea.

Please realise that you are helping your student to cope with their anxieties simply by teaching them kendo. Brad Binder contends most studies agree that regular participation in a martial art "cultivates decreases in hostility, anger, and feeling vulnerable to attack. They also lead to more easy-going and warm-hearted individuals and increases in self-confidence, self-esteem and self-control." This may in part be due to the fact that,

> "Asian martial arts have traditionally emphasized self-knowledge, self-improvement, and self-control. Unlike Western sports, Asian martial arts usually: teach self-defence, involve philosophical and ethical teachings to be applied to life, have a high degree of ceremony and ritual, emphasize the integration of mind and body, and have a meditative component." (Binder, 2007)

Should a student indicate that they are having a panic attack, take them aside. Remove them from class, but do not leave them alone. Have them sit down on the floor against a wall to prevent injuries should they faint. Guide them through a breathing exercise as described in the previous paragraph. Reassure them that they are safe and that, while it feels scary, they will be just fine. Help them dispel illogical anxious thoughts. Funny kendo stories are always great as backup material.

Finally, I would suggest that you keep on challenging these students. Continued exposure, by drawing them outside of their comfort zone, will hopefully help them extend beyond their limitations. Having responsibilities and being physically exhausted can lead to anxiety in these people, but being exposed to them in a supportive environment can also be therapeutic.

GAD in the Dojo: For Students

If you have GAD, or another anxiety disorder, I think you should first and foremost extend your support structure into the dojo. Inform your sensei of your issues because they have a need to know. As was discussed by Sheppard (2010), dojo staff need to be made aware of the medical conditions of their students, for their own safety. If there is a chance of you hyperventilating, fainting or having a panic attack during class, they need to know.

If you are on medication for your anxieties, please also inform your sensei. They do not necessarily have to know which medication it is, but they need to be made aware of possible side effects. They should also be able to inform emergency personnel if something ever happens to you.

If you feel comfortable enough to do so, confide in at least one *sempai* about your anxieties. They don't have to know everything about it, but talking about your thoughts and worries can help you calm down and put things into perspective. They can also take you aside during class if need be, so the rest of the class can proceed undisturbed and so you will not feel like the centre of attention.

Being prepared can give you a lot of peace of mind. I bring a first-aid kit with me to the dojo that includes a bag to breathe into (for hyperventilation) and some dextrose tablets. I also look up information about the dojo and tournament venues I will be visiting, to know about amenities, locations etc.

If you are not already in therapy, I would sincerely suggest CBT as it is able to help you understand your anxiety disorder and provide you with numerous tools to cope. Anxiety is not something that is easily cured, but by having the right skills under your belt you can definitely make life a lot easier for yourself!

And let me just say: kudos to you! You have already faced your anxieties and crossed your own boundaries by joining a kendo dojo. The toughest, loudest and smelliest martial art I know!

References
- Binder, B. *Psychosocial Benefits of the Martial Arts: Myth or Reality?*, 2007 (Retrieved from http://ftp.pwp.att.net/w/a/wabokujujitsu/articles/psychsoc.htm, 2013)
- Budden, P. *Buteyko and Kendo: My Personal Experience*, 2007 (Retrieved from http://www.kodokankendo.org/articles/techincal/199-buteyko-and-kendo-my-personal-experience, 2013)
- Buyens, G. *Glossary Related to BUDO and KOBUDO*, 2012 (Retrieved from www.hontaiyoshinryu.be, 2013)
- Rowney, J., Hermida, T. and Malone, D. *Anxiety Disorders, Cleveland Clinic*, 2010 (Retrieved from http://www.clevelandclinicmeded.com/medicalpubs/diseasemanagement/psychiatry-psychology/anxiety-disorder/, 2013)
- Salmon, G. *Kigurai*, 2009 (Retrieved from http://kendoinfo.wordpress.com/2009/04/07/kigurai/ 2013)
- Sheppard, B. "Teaching Kendo to Children" in *Kendo World 5.2*, pp.39-43, Chiba: Bunkasha International, 2010
- van Boeijen, C. *Begeleide Zelfhulp – overwinnen van angstklachten*, 2007 (Retrieved from http://www.vanboeijen.com 2013)

Getting to Grips with Who You Are

By Sakae Eri, Osaka University of Health and Sport Sciences
Translated by Paul Benson

Introduction

I decided to study psychology initially because I have a frail mind, and worry a lot because of it. I wanted to know what I could do to feel better. By writing this article I hope it helps me feel a little better about the troubles I face in the course of my daily life. For instance, I worry about personal relationships, and get depressed when I cannot perform to the best of my ability in competitions. I also hope this article will also be of use to other people who have similar anxieties.

My Own Perspective

In everyday life, there are countless people who lack confidence who think things like "I hate myself", "I'm no good", or "I don't know what to do". Such thoughts are certain to manifest, for example, when competitions do not go well, when you cannot find work, or when you encounter conflict in personal relationships.

Close examination of feelings like "I'm lacking" or "I'm inadequate" reveals that this is actually not the case at all. People without self-confidence often fall into a downward spiral in which the more they try to fix a weakness, the more intense it becomes. From a desire to succeed, they find reasons why they are likely to fail. From wanting to be validated, they end up focusing on their shortcomings. To use kendo as an example, this would be feelings of weak-spiritedness and pessimism after losing a *shiai* that you desperately wanted to win.

A way to escape this situation is to accept who you are, and the way you are. This is not easy. To put it another way, it may mean actually acknowledging that you are deficient in some things, and that you do not have high expectations of yourself. Some might say that this is counterproductive, but it is different from thinking you are a good-for-nothing loser. When you yield to yourself, recognise your weaknesses, and place no unrealistic expectations on yourself, you are not giving up; you come to see your strengths and gain leeway to actually believe in your potential. You facilitate progress by first becoming comfortable with, rather than pressurising yourself.

Once I was injured before a *shiai*, and my *keiko* was hopeless. At the time, my teacher said, "If you're injured, just put everything into what you CAN do. It's okay to not force yourself to do more." Up until then, I felt depressed, agonising over what to do. I also criticised myself, and gave myself no room to move. My teacher's words gave me some reprieve, and I was able to do *keiko* with a more positive attitude. I was at a standstill, but through acknowledging my difficulties, I was able to move forward little by little. This acknowledgment brought about progress.

"Accepting one's self = Being able to see one's potential"

By and large, people lack self-confidence when they are troubled, worried, or things do not go as expected. People who see their own deficiencies when compared to others should first try to write their troubles down on paper, i.e. what they are worried about, and what it was that did not go according to plan. Carefully looking at what is written, the writer will eventually come to realise that the critical issue is the gap between perception (self ideal) and reality. The trouble is the ideal—a desire of how things should be.

More than one's honest feelings, it is an ideal resting on judgments about the world and friends. However, many things do not go as expected in reality which is why it is troubling when the gap manifests. When you focus on these troubles, your attention shifts to what is missing; you see your deficiencies and what you lack. It is difficult to see what you have when your attention is on what you do not. At this point, you feel a massive shortcoming in yourself, and your self-confidence evaporates. When you are depressed, the first step is to consciously focus on and notice what you do possess. It is critical to shift your focus from what you lack to what you have.

"It's what you have, not what you lack"

Within us there is a mental barrier that diminishes our self-assuredness. It makes us think "that person is awful", "the world is a terrible place", and encourages us to blame our own troubles on somebody else. The unpleasant things that happen to us are not through bad luck, misfortune, or failure. They are what they are. If we are overly sensitive to them, we will lose our place at the helm of our lives. To make our lives enjoyable and pleasant, the question is how we can accept the reality before our eyes? I imagine that the answer is within us because the problems are too. I think that if we are aware of and stop our negative reaction to various problems we are faced with, the problems will fade away.

"Be aware of yourself, and the problems within will disappear naturally"

Athletes have mood fluctuations, and those who work to master something can experience temporary declines in technique—these are common to everyone. Some things we want to avoid, but generally we must go through them if we want to rise above where we are. Sometimes we must force ourselves through, and sometimes it is important to pause and think. By changing your frame of mind slightly, and recognising who you are, I think we can ease our moods and move in a positive direction.

Thinking from an Instructor's Perspective

I have written my own thoughts up to this point. Now I would like to consider the instructor's position, and offer advice on what to say to a troubled student who cannot perform to the best of their ability. This also applies to people in supportive roles, not just the instructor.

There is no right answer to this problem. Among students, there are some who want to listen and some who do not. There are at least as many opinions as there are students. I believe that the instructor must regularly try to grasp the student's character and opinions. It is important for the instructor to notice changes in the student's condition. One phrase a teacher should avoid with troubled students is simply saying "*gambare*" (try hard). To the speaker, it is an innocent phrase said only for encouragement, but it often puts great pressure on the listener: it can also hurt them depending on the time and situation. Seemingly harmless words are often fraught with underlying complications.

Instead, instructors should avoid phrases that rush or pressure a troubled student, and strive to create an environment where the student can progress at his or her own pace. However, as I wrote in the introduction, each student is different, and reacts differently, so instructors should try to respond suitably to each. It is important to create an accommodating environment and atmosphere.

Instructors are in a position in which they must try to understand each student, and it should be noted that it is extraordinarily difficult to take a role in alleviating a person's mental or psychological issues.

"To understand someone, you first need to understand yourself"

Conclusion

It is possible to reflect on who we are through being calm, changing our attitude, and acknowledging who we are. I also believe it is possible to hold a compassionate attitude towards others. When you have experienced suffering, you notice and understand the feelings of others who suffer in a similar way. I believe it is important to expand our perspectives and notice the feelings of those around us. This happens through "noticing one's self, understanding one's self, and controlling one's self." The importance of this cannot be overstated.

While there are differences in the severity of our problems, such as the conflicts in our personal relationships, temporary lapses in technique, and troubles in daily life, it is safe to say that changing our mind-set and accepting the self is connected to everything.

In considering and researching this topic, I met people who think and perceive things very differently. While there is no one-size-fits-all solution, I found that there is a fitting answer for each different situation. When I meet someone who is worried and troubled, I want to be able to offer advice that is appropriate to that individual, and also be someone with compassion who can empathise with their feelings. It is my hope that this short essay will be useful in some way to those who read it.

A Cognitive Neuroscience Perspective on 'Enzan-no-Metsuke'

By Taylor Winter, Michael Wrigley, and Darryl Tong

An interesting problem in kendo is the tendency for practitioners to focus on specific features or aspects of their opponent instead of observing them as a whole. Such a tendency is the consequence of our ability to selectively attend to stimuli in an automatic and rapid manner (Gazzaniga, Ifry, and Mangun, 2009). In the intermediate levels of kendo, our attention system can lead us to focus on a target (i.e. *kote*), rather than the entire person in front of us. Beginners exhibit the same problem, but one which is exacerbated by focusing only on the opponent's *shinai*. Although our attention system is incredibly well adapted, these scenarios illustrate the pitfalls in our cognitive response to an opponent.

In kendo there is the teaching "*enzan-no-metsuke*" (looking at a far mountain), which helps practitioners develop a more holistic sense of attention. It teaches that the practitioner should look upon their opponent as a whole, without focusing on one particular area. It therefore makes them able to see any changes that manifest themselves in the opponent. In reality, however, in the early stages of kendo a beginner tends to predominantly focus on what the *shinai* is doing, and not much else. With more training and experience, we can learn through conscious effort to override this automaticity of initial selective attention.

William James, in his book *Principles of Psychology* (1890), defined attention as "the taking possession by the mind, in clear and vivid form, of one out of what seem several simultaneously possible objects or trains of thought. Focalization, concentration, of consciousness are of its essence." It highlights why we encounter difficulty when attempting to take a more holistic approach to attention in kendo. Selective attention is best understood as a focus on a single stream of incoming information out of many.

In selective attention, the selection of information involves two subset mechanisms: target amplification and distractor inhibition (Wyatt & Machado, 2013). Target amplification is a boost to the incoming signal of information to allow us to focus ourselves, for example on a potential or real immediate threat (i.e. the *shinai*). Distractor inhibition decreases the information flow of everything beyond the amplified stream (i.e. the person holding the *shinai* or their movement and intentions). Amplification of attention to a *shinai* may not be significantly detrimental, and perhaps in some ways might be an advantage. However, when coupled with the inhibition of everything else regarding the opponent, this cumulative effect completely numbs our ability to engage the opponent as a whole entity.

Current theories in cognitive neuroscience indicate that individuals (particularly beginners) want to look at the *shinai* and not 'at a far mountain'. There is research to support this concept in forensic crime. In the area of eyewitness testimony, a witness' memory is severely impacted when a weapon is present during a crime. This is because the presentation of a weapon draws their attention to the weapon and not the person holding it. This is referred to as 'weapon focus', and demonstrates why kendo practitioners might be predisposed to selectively attend to a *shinai* rather than a holistic representation of an opponent.

Loftus, Loftus, and Messo (1987) demonstrated the weapon focus effect in a laboratory setting using eye movement tracking. Thirty-six study participants were divided into two groups. One group viewed a video of a customer walking into a restaurant and presenting a cheque that was exchanged for cash. A second group of participants saw a similar video except a gun was shown instead of a chequebook. Participants in the weapon group looked at the gun more often and for a longer period than those who were presented with a chequebook. The second group were also significantly less likely to recall other details of the situation, and were far less likely to recall the perpetrator's appearance. In this instance the gun has a similar effect to that of a *shinai* in kendo. Similar studies have replicated the paradigm of Loftus et al. (1987) using knives, a more direct analogy to kendo, that has produced the weapon focus effect to a higher degree.

The reasoning behind weapon focus is that we utilise selective attention to focus towards objects of arousal or potential danger in terms of self-preservation (Hope and Wright, 2006). Consider a tennis ball unexpectedly thrown at you with the appropriate arousal elicited due to the potential of the tennis ball to hit you. Attention is given to the ball using target amplification and our cognitive resources are dedicated to dodging the ball or catching it. The person who threw the ball is superfluous and incoming information regarding the thrower is inhibited as would occur with a gun, knife, or *shinai*.

Weapon focus is very likely to be the cause of kendo practitioners selectively attending on *shinai*. The stage of focusing on a *shinai* in a kendoka's career is short-lived, however. Remarkably, we can suppress the effect of weapon focus reasonably quickly, which frees us to gather more information from our opponent, information that would otherwise be classed as distracting and therefore inhibited. Some research suggests that kendoka may desensitise over time with repeated exposure to an opponent with a *shinai* (Pickel, 1999). The *shinai* becomes less arousing and so the effect of weapon focus is reduced.

Pickel (1999) showed participants images of either a priest or a police officer carrying either a gun or a cell phone. Participants were far less accurate at describing the priest with a gun relative to the police officer. Multiple exposures to a police officer with a gun mediated the effect of weapon focus allowing for an accurate description. A priest carrying a gun is far less common and so participants found the gun arousing and shifted their attention accordingly. Information regarding the priest's appearance was inhibited and description accuracy significantly decreased. Analogous to this study, kendoka begin by encountering their opponent as participants in Pickel's study encountered the priest. As a pairing of an opponent with a *shinai* becomes more natural, kendoka start to view their opponent as Pickel's participants viewed the police officer.

Essentially, the presented cognitive framework supports the importance of adhering to *enzan-no-metsuke*, as if looking at a far mountain in order to encompass all its features. In *Gorin-no-sho* (1645, trans. Wilson, 2002), Miyamoto Musashi developed a similar theory. He said that there were two ways of looking: "*kan*" (observation) and "*ken*" (seeing). Briefly, *kan* is more holistic, to see the near as the far, and far as near, to not be distracted by the opponent's sword. *Ken* deals with superficial details (i.e. exclusively visual) and is therefore weak, whereas *kan* is strong, which leads Musashi to contend that great efforts should be made in *kan*. Musashi's writings give a historical insight into an early understanding of selective attention, so it appears that the weapon focus effect was acknowledged as early as the seventeenth century in Japan.

Kendo is full of adages that have been tried and tested over centuries, but some still remain anecdotal. However, some of these teachings, when evaluated from an evidence-based standpoint, appear to stand up well to scientific scrutiny. Therefore, understanding some of these from a more scientific standpoint may allow for better teaching practice in the future, with the potential to modify teaching strategies at group or individual levels, in order to learn key concepts in kendo.

References

- Gazzaniga, M., Ivry, R. and Mangun, G. *Cognitive Neuroscience: The Biology of the Mind* (3rd ed.), New York: W.W. Norton & Company, 2009.
- Hope, L. and Wright, D. "Beyond Unusual? Examining the Role of Attention in the Weapon Focus Effect" in *Applied Cognitive Psychology*, 21, pp.951–961, 2007.
- James, W. *The Principles of Psychology* (2 vols.), New York: Henry Holt, 1890. (Reprinted Bristol: Thoemmes Press, 1999)
- Loftus, E., Loftus, G., & Messo, J. "Some Facts About 'Weapon Focus'" in *Law and Human Behavior*, 11(1), pp.55-62, 1983.
- Miyamoto, M. *Gorin-no-sho*, 1645 (trans Wilson, W. S., Boston, MA: Shambhala Publications, 2002)
- Pickel, K. L. "Distinguishing Eyewitness Descriptions of Perceived Objects from Descriptions of Imagined Objects" in *Applied Cognitive Psychology*, 13, pp.399–413, 1999.
- Wyatt N. and Machado L. "Evidence Inhibition Responds Reactively to the Salience of Distracting Information during Focused Attention" in *PLoS ONE*, 8(4), e62809, 2013.

RED SEA KENDO—Kendo in Israel

by Ido Slonimsky/Photographs by Erez Figlash

Participants of the seminar in Eilat

Emilio Gomez (K7-dan Kyoshi) and Roni Tira (3-dan) demonstrating Nippon Kendo Kata at the seminar

In March 2013, the sounds of *kiai* and *fumikomi* could be heard in the Red Sea city of Eilat, Israel. These were sounds that filled Israeli kenshi with pride, and have been a landmark in the progress of Israeli kendo. Kendo was first introduced to Israel in 1991, and at that time there were only ten practitioners. Many came and went during the 1990s, but a core group of people continued to practise, and slowly started to gain recognition from the European and international federations.

It was not until 2004 that Israel had its first kendo seminar, which was coordinated by Jean-Pierre Raick, kendo and iaido K7-dan, and technical director of the European Kendo Federation. At that time there were only two kendo clubs in Israel, one in Tel-Aviv led by Marco Edry, and the other in the northern town of Kiryat Tivon, led by Eyal Weiss, both of whom were 3-dan at the time.

Raick-sensei's seminar introduced the Israeli kenshi to a new level of kendo, and gave the participants a goal to strive for, and opened their eyes to kendo beyond their borders. Up until then, most members of the Israeli federation had never met anyone who practised kendo outside their own club, let alone someone from a different country. Raick-sensei has since come to Israel on a yearly basis, each time showing Israeli kenshi that kendo is a never-ending path of learning and self improvement.

The experience gained at these seminars changed the perception of kendo for Israeli kenshi, and made them eager to attain dan grades and attend worldwide seminars. Also, since there are not enough high ranking teachers in Israel to facilitate examinations there, Israeli kendoka have started to travel overseas to grade, and have started to meet and mingle with other European practitioners.

The road of progress has not been an easy one, but with the dedication and devotion that has characterised kendo in Israel since its beginnings, the Israeli Federation started to grow and eventually gained more *yūdansha* members. The Israeli federation started sending its *yūdansha* members to referee seminars and held its own small championships. Then in 2009, dan examinations were held in Israel for the first time.

In March 2013, thanks to Pasha Volodarsky, 4-dan and head of the kendo division within the Israeli Kendo Federation, kendo in Israel reached another milestone when it hosted its first large-scale international seminar and championship in the southernmost city of Eilat, which is located on the shores of the Red Sea. This seminar was led by K7-dan Emilio Gomez, who came from Belgium, and there were also participants from Austria, Norway, Ukraine and Russia. Such a large contingent of kenshi from different countries was a sight to behold for many of the Israeli participants. It brought a breath of fresh air into competition in Israel.

Gomez-sensei emphasised the importance of this unique gathering in Israel, and said that although the kenshi are from different nations they are all friends. He explained further that "*ichigan*" from the saying "*ichi-gan ni-soku san-tan shi-riki*" (first eyes, second feet, third gut, fourth power), means to look at your opponent with kindness, not with anger. This attitude was adopted by everyone, and with kendo in the day and beer at night, the gathering truly promoted friendship between all participants.

Another important factor of the seminar was that it was a step towards development of the next generation of Israeli kendoka. Young kenshi from the ages of 10 to 14 attended the seminar for the first time, practising side by side with their older colleagues. A junior competition was also held, with emphasis on good *ippon*, and not counting *jōgai* (stepping out of bounds) as *hansoku*. This brought out beautiful kendo from the juniors, as they did their best to perform big and correct *kihon*. This was followed by the team competition, which had many teams made up of participants from different countries – testament to the friendship created at this event.

A very high level was shown in the individual competition, and the final between Kawaharada Takanori (Israel) and Genady Dubilin (Russia) was very exciting to watch. In the end it was Genady Dubilin that won the championship, showing good spirit and technique in doing so.

The gathering at Eilat brought together many new friends, and gave Israeli kenshi new goals to work towards. With the federation already working on next year's event, we hope that we will meet again by the Red Sea, and watch the sunset over a cold beer knowing that the next morning we will be doing *keiko* again.

THE SPIRIT OF THE SAMURAI LIVES ON IN MONTREAL
The Collection of Dr. Richard Béliveau

By Gabriel Weitzner

"My fascination with the samurai began when I was 11 years old. Taking up the study of the martial arts, I entered a world of courage, perseverance, courtesy, respect, honour, simplicity and modesty. Ever since then, I have embraced these values. In my difficult moments, they have given me the strength to carry on."

Richard has also had the opportunity to visit Japan several times on business, and he spoke about an experience that he had in Japan.

"I remember strolling all alone through the gravestones one morning, shrouded in the thick dawn mist. The gravel crunched softly beneath my feet. I may have been in the centre of Tokyo, but the only sound I heard came from three crows perched in one of the pine trees. An elderly monk had lit thousands of incense sticks and their heady scent wafted through the air. Above all, I could feel the presence of the souls of those great samurai who had so readily sacrificed their lives. This was the Senkakuji Temple, where the 47 Ronin from one of Japan's best-loved legends are buried."

Dr. Richard Béliveau has a PhD in biochemistry, and is a professor of surgery, biochemistry and physiology at the Université du Quebec a Montreal. He has also authored over 250 publications in international medical journals. I first met him in Montreal in the early 1980s; I had arrived in Montreal in 1981 to conduct research at the Montreal Children's Hospital's Research Institute at McGill University, and also at the Royal Victoria Transplant Department. Richard and I developed a great friendship talking about research, practising kendo together at the small Shidokan Dojo, and sharing a few beers after practice. One Sunday morning, as we walked through downtown Montreal, Richard explained the origins of his interest in the samurai and the martial arts.

Over time Richard managed to acquire one of the world's largest, rarest and historically valuable collections of Japanese armour, helmets, masks, swords and spears. From May 17, 2012, to March 31, 2013, for the first time Richard exhibited some of his collection at the Montreal Museum of Archaeology and History in an exhibition called "Samurai - The Prestigious Collection of Richard Béliveau". What follows is a glimpse of his collection.

The main insignia on this set of armour proclaims that its owner was of the Arima Clan, and the secondary insignia is of the Tomoe. It clearly belonged to a wealthy samurai, as indicated by its tiny metal scales, the Chinese silk, the chased metal decorations and gold plating—some even hiding from view, under the shoulder guards for instance. The neckpiece and wristlets are inspired by Portuguese armour. The iron helmet has eight plates.

This *hoshi-bashi* helmet, made of 64 perfectly fitted plates with tiny extruding rivets, is decorated with gilded wings and an impressive glass-eyed demon.

The shield-like *ōsode* shoulder guards of this Edo period (1603-1868) set of armour are made of individual scales and resemble those of the very ancient and heavy *ō-yoroi* armour. The helmet is signed by Saotome Iechika, a very prestigious armourer.

Elegant simplicity: this armour seems to be made of individual scales, but if you were to look at the back of the cuirass, you see a series of metal lames with saw-tooth top edges. These lames are called imitation scales.

A treasure of its time: The surface of the elegant imitation-scale armour shows that it saw much wear. It was made in the late Azuchi Momoyama period (1573–1600). Atop the mask with its splendid moustache sits a helmet of the Saika school, thought to have been active between 1550–1650, and which specialised in making multi-plate helmets. This one has six plates.

Eye catching orange: This monochrome armour is from the Azuchi Momoyama period. Its orange colour is similar to that of the armour illustrated on scrolls from this period. The *suji-bashi* helmet has 62 plates, held in place by numerous rivets called *ko-boshi* (little stars).

A terrifying dragon: Making and lacing scale armour was a very lengthy process. To keep up with demand as wars proliferated, sixteenth century armourers devised a new type of armour. The cuirass was now made of wider laced or riveted lames. This new style met with great success. It was lighter, easier to make and faster to repair, and had fewer holes in the metal.

A demonic mask: this set of armour with a helmet dating from the Muromachi period (1336–1573), is made of laced metal lames, including the cuirass beneath its leather guard, and paired with a splendid *mempo karasu* mask. Its wealthy owner was a *hatamoto*, the high-ranking samurai under the shogun's command, who carried the banners on the battlefield. The prestigious insignia show that its owner served Toyotomi Hideyoshi.

Kaga suits of armour: *kaga* armour was produced by the Unkai school of armourers, founded in the second half of the seventeenth century by the swordsmith Unkai Mitsunao. The school served the Maeda family, the *daimyō* of Kanazawa in Kaga, Japan's richest province, until the end of the Edo period. On the cuirass of this *kaga* set of armour, there is a Sanskrit character that represents Shiva, one of the three main Hindu gods, who symbolises both destruction and creation. The *mempo* mask is signed Myochin Munetaka. The 16 plate *suji-bashi* helmet with its large rivets, is also of the Kaga school.

Tachi over 60 cm: this *tachi* mounting from the Meiji period (1868–1912) holds a blade forged in about the mid-fifteenth century in a Bizen school workshop, the source of more than half of all swords recognised as Japanese National Treasures. The hilt of the sword is covered with ray skin.

Katana: the lacquer on the scabbard of this long *katana* resembles cherry bark. At the end of the hilt, the pommel cap shows a samurai dressed in armour. The very valuable blade was forged by Masatoshi between 1555 and 1558.

The length and sharply curved blade of a *tachi* developed from the Heian period (794–1185) and allowed warriors to strike enemies from horseback. These cavalry swords were also worn by nobles of the court and could be richly decorated. This one is adorned with a silver phoenix. The hilt, normally unwrapped, was covered by ray skin, and the shape of the hand guard was still close to that of some Mongol and Chinese swords.

The rise of the *tachi* marked the advent of the great Japanese swords. The quality of the blade improved, the scabbards were decorated and coloured, often with vermilion, and the fittings became intricately detailed. Next to evolve would be the *katana*. The blade attributed to Chiyozuru was forged in the late seventeenth century in Echizen, one of the major production centres. It shows the shift from *tachi* to *katana* and *wakizashi*. Although it has a tachi shape, the point is already longer and rounder.

This suit of armour is one of the finest of the collection, made by the Unkai school. There are a number of clues to the wealth of the samurai who commissioned it, the use of leather with European motifs, imported from far-off Holland, the cuirass with its repousse lion uchidachi and the richly decorated visor. Donning this armour was a way of telling the whole world that you were rich and powerful. The armour is signed on the underside of the simplest component, the shin guards, that suggests a very Zen reserve.

Acknowledgments: I would like express my gratitude to Dr. Richard Béliveau for taking the time to share his thoughts, knowledge and time for this article. For those who would like to follow Dr. Béliveau's research, he has published the following books: *Foods That Fight Cancer*; *Cooking with Foods That Fight Cancer*; *Eating Well, Living Well*; and *Death: The Scientific Facts to Help Us Understand It*.

NAGINATA TOURNAMENT SIMULATION
A Method for Training Tournament Staff

By Kurt Schmucker

In Japan there are naginata tournaments held almost every week, so there are abundant opportunities for competitors, referees, officials, and organisers to sharpen their skills. In the US, however, there are only a handful of tournaments each year, so the opportunities for tournament training are relatively rare. While competitors can practise their *shiai* skills in their local dojo, what can record-keepers and other organisers do to make sure that the tournament is properly recorded? Examples of the forms used to record tournaments in naginata are shown in Fig. 1 and Fig. 2 (see the end of the article), and these can be imposing to a record-keeper with little experience.

This article describes a technique to simulate naginata tournaments for record-keepers and other tournament staff that requires only a pencil, paper, and a few dice. An entire day-long tournament can be simulated in less than two hours, and in this way, staff who do the record keeping associated with a tournament can get a great deal of practice in a small amount of time. The randomness of the dice provides a level of excitement and unpredictability that also makes the simulation fun. The simulation parameters have been chosen so that a realistic tournament is generated, thereby making the experience relevant to staff training.

This staff training technique has been used in the US and Canada a number of times, and has proven to be effective, efficient, and fun.

Basic Operation

This simulation assumes that a tournament ladder already exists (the easiest thing to do is just to re-use one from a previous championship). To conduct a match, dice are used to determine significant events like the awarding of a point, the imposition of a penalty, the expiration of time, *etc*. For *shiai* tournaments, three dice are thrown and the sum of the values shown is used with a table to determine the next significant action in the simulated match. It is this table that is key to the simulation working (there is a different table used for *engi* [naginata form competitions] and for *shiai*). These events are then entered onto the appropriate forms by the staff recording the simulation, just as they would in a real tournament. The simulation continues until the champion is decided. The exact manner in which these events are recorded is regularly checked, to make sure the staff who are recording the simulated tournament are doing so correctly.

Engi Tournaments

An *engi* tournament is particularly easy to simulate using just a single die and the following table, since the only event that needs to be simulated is the resulting decision of the five referees:

Die Value	Engi Match Result
1	5 flags for red; 0 flags for white
2	4 flags for red; 1 flag for white
3	3 flags for red; 2 flags for white
4	2 flags for red; 3 flags for white
5	1 flag for red; 4 flags for white
6	0 flags for red; 5 flags for white

Each of the six events in this table are equally likely to occur, which results in a reasonable approximation of a real *engi* tournament.

Shiai Tournaments

There are many more types of events in a *shiai* tournament than in an *engi* one. To properly choose these events in a simulated tournament so that the various probabilities closely approximate a real naginata tournament, a number of different events were tabulated from two recent United States Naginata Federation (USNF) tournaments,[1] with the following results:

Event	Total Occurrences
Sune scored	89
Men scored	15
Match time limit reached	15
Hansoku committed	14
Match defaulted (*Fusenshō* or injury)	1
Kote scored	1
Tsuki scored	0
Dō scored	0

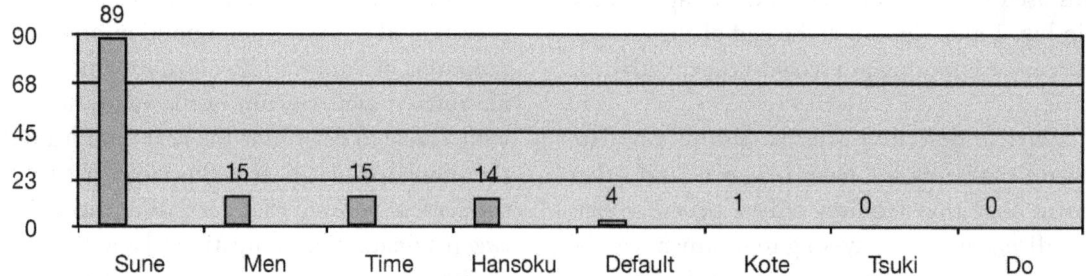

---

[1] The Sixth USNF Championship (Honolulu in 2000) and the Eighth USNF Championship (Bryn Mawr in 2004)

There is a range of three to 18 for the total when using three dice. These values do not occur with the same probability, but rather with the following relative probabilities [2]:

Total (3 dice)	Relative Probability
3	1
4	3
5	6
6	10
7	15
8	21
9	25
10	27
11	27
12	25
13	21
14	15
15	10
16	6
17	3
18	1

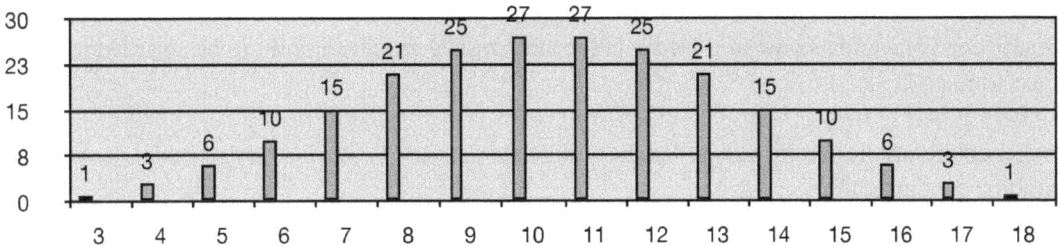

Using the two tables above as guides, and attempting to both (1) approximately match the relative frequency of events in real *shiai* tournaments, and (2) ensure that even rare events (e.g., a *dō* point scored) occur once in a while in the simulated tournament so that the staff recording it will get a wide range of experience, the following table was created. It has worked well to produce realistic and useful tournament simulations:

Total (3 dice)	Event
3	Dō by White
4	Tsuki by White
5	Default by White
6	Kote by White
7	Match time limit reached
8	Men by White
9	Hansoku by White
10	Sune by White
11	Sune by Red
12	Hansoku by Red
13	Men by Red
14	(Simulation Director's choice)
15	Kote by Red
16	Default by Red
17	Tsuki by Red
18	Dō by Red

---

[2] This assumes that standard six-sided (cubic) dice are used. Dice with more than six sides (e.g., dodecahedral or icosahedral dice) would not work well for this simulation technique.

Typically, one individual (the simulation director) will hand out the tournament ladder and the blank forms used to record the results of the matches, throw the dice, and call out the tournament events and other appropriate referee calls i.e. "*Sune* by red!"; "*Kote* by red!"; "*Shōbu ari!*". The simulation director will also make sure that everyone involved knows which match is being run, and will regularly double-check that the various forms are being filled out correctly. There are several special situations in the above table that the simulation director must deal with:

Hansoku—To increase the realism of the simulation, the director can call out specific fouls when a *hansoku* is generated i.e. *jōgai* (out of bounds), *naginata otoshi* (dropping a *naginata*), etc.

Default—How a default is dealt with depends on the state of the tournament and the match. A default that occurs in the first tournament round and before any player has been awarded a point or committed a violation can be announced as a *fusenshō* (a win because the opponent did not show up). In other cases, a default can be announced as an injury.

Match time limit reached—How a match time limit event is dealt with depends on the state of the match and the tournament rules. This could be an *ippon-gachi* (win by one point), an *enchō*, or a *hantei*. This depends on the tournament rules, whether it is the championship match, etc. In the case of *hantei*, one more throw of the dice can determine the match winner.

Simulation Director's choice—Generally, the simulation director will be an experienced referee or tournament official. When this event is rolled, the director can use his or her judgment to announce any event that will make the simulation more interesting (a match time limit event to force an *enchō* if one has not occurred recently; a point to cause a team tie, and thus force a playoff match; etc.) or to cause a somewhat rare event to make sure everyone knows how to record it (a second *hansoku* causing a point to be awarded to the opponent, or a rare foul).

In addition, the simulation director can add some additional colourful commentary to make the simulation more enjoyable. Some examples are:

1. When the dice throw is a 10 (*sune* by white), instead of just saying, "*Sune* by white," say, "Mike stumbles, falls to the floor, but comes up fighting, scoring a *sune* from *wakigamae*! The spectators stand and cheer wildly!";

2. When the dice throw is 9 (*hansoku* by white) instead of saying, "*Hansoku* by white," say, "Kurt scares John out of the *shiai-jō* for the second time; *hansoku* by white, *ippon* for red. *Shōbu*-ari!" Such comments, if well done, can make the simulation mimic the excitement of a real *shiai*.

Conclusion

This simulation technique has been successfully used to train naginata tournament officials in the Northern California Naginata Federation, the United States Naginata Federation and the Canadian Naginata Federation. It has proven to be educational, useful, enjoyable and engaging.

This simulation could easily be adopted for the training of tournament officials in kendo, judo, and other martial arts, by gathering the data on actual events in several real tournaments and by adapting the tables that are the heart of the simulation technique.

Kurt Schmucker is the vice-president of the United States Naginata Federation and has been active at the national and international levels in naginata for more than 18 years. He holds the following ranks: 5-dan in naginata and iaido, 4-dan in kendo, 3-dan in jodo, and *oku-iri* in Shindo Muso-ryū Jōjutsu.

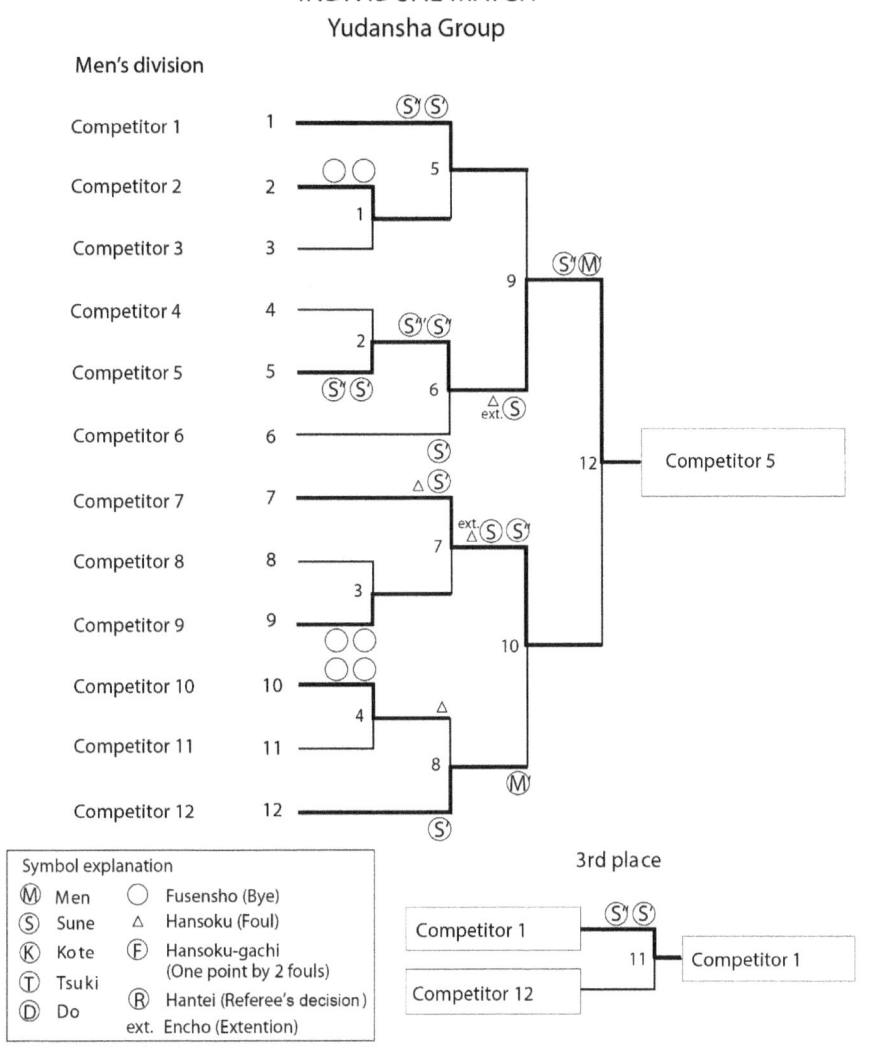

Fig. 1. A tournament ladder with the additional markings used to record the results of a naginata tournament.

Fig. 2. The form used to record a naginata team match, complete with all the markings for each individual match, as well as the result of the team match.

Shinai Saga
Duelling Ground

By Charlie Kondek

A five minute break in *keiko* had been called, long enough to catch one's breath after the intense drills of *mawari-geiko* and *kakari-geiko*, to adjust the *himo* on the *men* or the wrap and fold of the *tenugui*, to inspect *shinai*, steal a drink or scratch one's nose (for some, with a bamboo implement thrust between the bars of the *mengane*). Myriad small noises accompanied this, and to Mazurski they resembled an orchestra warming up, final preparations for a symphony of uncertain carnage. Muttered conversations in English and Japanese carpeted the wide, dry gym beneath shuffling feet, heavy breathing, a laugh here and there, the sound of zippered compartments being opened, clasps unbuttoned, cords pulled taut snap, snap. Mazurski did not adjust his *men*. It felt a little loose, but he knew from experience that if he tightened it over his sweat-slick head it would slip too tightly and cause him irritating discomfort midway through the *ji-geiko* section. He did not pace as he waited. Rather, he stood still and concentrated on drawing deep, silent breaths.

Refreshed, equipped, the assembled swordsmen took to their feet and began to gather on the practice floor. They fell into pairs. There was a mixed group this evening, with several people from Ogawara-sensei's dojo in attendance, though not Ogawara-sensei himself. Mazurski moved to stand opposite Ando, the visiting 5-dan, but was a step behind Nygaard, who got there first. Instead, he found himself across from Coyle, a guy at his own 2-dan level. As he waited for the others to align, Mazurski made a silent vow to himself, to use this time to concentrate on a number of fundamentals—to fight hard and to take *ippon*, of course—but also to work on a personal list of habits that included lowering his *kensen*, keeping his feet from drifting too far apart, attacking with the lower body as opposed to leading with the arms, and keeping his right hand reigned in.

It was to be a rotating *ji-geiko*, Nygaard explained. Ando-sensei would stay in the *shōmen* corner and everyone would rotate past his fixed position. Each match would be about three to five minutes. Mazurski was still concentrating on himself, faintly aware of Coyle, but another part of him wondered who in this group he would fence tonight, and the kinds of challenges posed by each pairing. Once again as they bowed from the waist with a loud "*Onegai shimasu*!", stepped to the centre, crossed swords and took the *sonkyo* position, Mazurski was reminded of an orchestra preparing to play. Each instrument was readied, the conductor paused, his baton aloft. It would be a harsh, arrhythmic piece, a theme of action in several movements. "*Hajime!*" The angry *kiai* from those assembled, first one, then another, then more, were its opening notes.

Mazurski and Coyle stood and launched themselves at each other's *men* at exactly the same time and with the same effect; a harmonious explosion of bamboo. They pressed. Mazurski circled to his left. They placed *shinai* on each other's shoulders and separated cautiously. "Shouldn't let him do that," Mazurski thought, eyeing the *kensen* of his opponent. "Or me. Should try *hiki-waza*." Now their swords crossed again and Mazurski acknowledged consciously his other tasks—keep the *kensen* low, keep the feet together, push the left hand out with the lower body. Coyle was coming in again, wanted that *men* again, Mazurski would give it to him. Again their swords crossed in flight and he was conscious of the scent of burnt wood as their bodies slammed together following the simultaneous cut.

What was it he said? No relaxing. Seek the opportunity for *hiki-waza*. They'd recently been working on the footwork for this, and so Mazurski moved his left foot back, pushed with his hips and wrists, tried to read which way Coyle would jump—he pushed his *tsuka* into Coyle's, used the push to lift his hands, snapped down with hand and foot. A pop on the *men-buton* rewarded him as he rocketed backwards.

Fighting Coyle, for Mazurski, was like fighting a mirror. They were the same level in ability and skill, had the same temperament, the same impatient need for action. They threw *waza* at each other one after the next without much eye to cause and effect, without anticipation of what the other would do, but only with a set of preferences for the *waza* at which they excelled—mostly fast, small *men*, *kote* and *kote-men*. After setting the pace with an exchange of several *ai-waza*, they now began to attempt more calculation: what can I do that will occur at the same time as his attack but just ahead of his, so that mine lands first? Can I attack *men* just a little faster? Is now the time to try for *de-gote*? Neither Mazurski nor Coyle were particularly suited to this style of fighting, so while some *ippon* were scored by both, it showed only the germ of the higher communication possible between them. Instead of "what will he do?" the focus was on cutting faster, faster, beating the other man—not to the punch, but to the cut. Mazurski quite forgot his footwork in his zeal.

At a loud cry from Nygaard, keeping time in his head, it was over, and Mazurski thanked Coyle, and rotated to his left, to the opponent he'd originally sought, Ando. The atmosphere changed. It was a resetting of the tempo. As Mazurski bowed from the waist and approached he was conscious of the difference in skill, and he was thinking of how he might fend off catastrophe, what extraordinary moves he might make to counter an opponent whose skill exceeded his. He was conscious, in this fight, in a way he had not been fighting Coyle.

This duel was slower. Ando took the centre, the tip of his *shinai* inches from Mazurski's, just out of range for both. Ando's *kiai* seemed to hold something back, to promise something more. Mazurski emptied his lungs in response. He wanted to step in and cut but did not. Why didn't he? He sensed a trap, sensed, somehow, that he couldn't simply do what he preferred to do, try to bludgeon Ando. He doubted himself. He didn't know it, but it was Ando's *seme* that held him.

Mazurski took a big breath, took one step in, crossing swords with Ando. Now, he thought, drive in more, push Ando's centre aside, clear the path to *men*. But something was wrong—had Ando moved a shade to the left, or was it only that he had pressed Mazurski's *shinai* down? Both *shinai* rose along the same trajectory as each fencer suddenly leaped forward, but when the cuts were completed Ando's struck Mazurski's *men* while Mazurski's found only empty air somewhere past Ando's left ear. Mazurski felt as if standing still while Ando drove through and past him.

Mazurski gathered his breath and tried again. Now he remembered his fundamentals. He concentrated on Ando's eyes. If facing Coyle was like facing a mirror, this was like facing a wall. But Mazurski would find a way through the wall, was certain he could find one, that it was not beyond his skill. He knew, too, that this is what Ando was leading him to do, was how he was teaching him. Ando's fencing said to Mazurski, "That didn't work. Try again. Come on." Both fencers fought for the centre between them.

Mazurski pulled breath into his lungs and pressed forward with his back foot driving. He began to fall toward Ando's *tsuki*, and against his pliant *shinai*, but tried to hold it, hold it, to see if there was a reaction from Ando, something opening—damn, he was inscrutable, and Mazurski was passing a point at which he could not change his mind, so he resolved in a fraction of an instant to put everything he had into it, committing completely to the attack. As his right foot took flight he felt the sting of Ando's *kote*, saw his *men* stab ineffectually at the air inches above and to the right of Ando's *men*. Their bodies collided. Mazurski's body stopped where it was. Ando's bounced and circled away, taking *ippon* with it.

Mazurski never did find a way through Ando's wall. The closest he came was a couple of exchanges of *ai-men* that sent both *shinai* astray, neither a victory. Ando nodded once or twice when Mazurski was close or had done something effective, but he let his combat do the bulk of the instruction. It seemed to say, "What you normally do will not work on me. There's something you're missing. You have to figure it out. No, that's not it. Keep trying." Mazurski was no closer to the solution when the match ended and, thanking Ando, he circled around him and to the next place.

Mazurski allowed a moment of chagrin to surface when he saw that he now faced McCandless. The effort of fighting Ando had pushed him temporarily to the limits of his mental as well as physical endurance, and now, with McCandless, a *mudansha*-level fighter and still a beginner, Mazurski would have to fight in a way that was instructive; he would have to fight at a level just above McCandless, who would attack frequently, repeatedly, with big *men* cuts. Mazurski would have to keep up, set a good example. And he was tired.

Now he concentrated on breathing from the stomach, and the left foot. McCandless was on his third match, too, but breathing fire, and he did not disappoint Mazurski when he attacked right away with a big *men* cut. Mazurski answered in kind, and their *shinai* found the targets together and at once. Mazurski wondered if he could practise his *hiki-waza* on McCandless. He could, he made it ring—he would have to explain later to McCandless how he did it, teach him. Now again, a large, thundering *ai-men*, McCandless growing stronger, holding more of the centre. Mazurski forced conscious control over his breathing, pulled his left foot closer to his right heel. He decided to shift his timing, cut a bit sooner—he would show McCandless, too, how to take *kote*, by taking his *kote*.

Somehow, by the time his match with McCandless was over, Mazurski had regained his stamina, was back in the game. Who was next? Who else would he fence that evening?

Yun, whose kendo was just a shade better than Mazurski's, who seemed to take three *ippon* for every one of his.

Tamanaha, one of the kids, for whom Mazurski would mostly crouch and receive, encouraging the boy to use his *kiai* and commit completely to the cut in such a way as to make the *shinpan* flags stand up.

Blythe, a prolific blocker and dodger. His method was to stifle each attack thrown at him until the opponent got frustrated, paused—and allowed Blythe an instant to take *men* or *kote*, usually while the opponent was still backing up. On a good day, Mazurski could turn Blythe's blocking against him, pressure *men*, provoke the block, open *kote* for the taking. On a good day.

He'd fight Nygaard, his friend and coach, whose kendo he knew so well. He'd push their rivalry further, pursue Nygaard closer at his heels, take at least one *ippon* that was the ransom paid the teacher by the student.

He'd fight Mrs. Tamanaha, mother of the boy, who had skill but lacked confidence, in whom he would encourage a proud, competitive spirit. She was most comfortable fighting other women. Mazurski wanted to tell her: "You're as good as me. Take my *men*! Take my *kote*!"

Mazurski would fight them all, and they would fight each other. Each pairing would be a unique puzzle, a riddle to be solved by each participant: how do I, with my assets, take *ippon* from this person, with his assets? They would fill the room with noise, fill it to its high rafters, air ducts and halogen lights. They would skirmish to the last "*yame!*" and afterward fall gratefully into panting *seiza*. In *mokusō*, Mazurski would wonder if he had done all he could, if he had kept to his list of checkpoints, if he had addressed his fundamentals. Had he recalled and applied the words of his various sensei? Was he recalling them now? It would dissolve, these thoughts, in the bathing breath of the *mokusō*. He would leave it, for the moment, "on the floor," as he'd been taught to do.

But then, bowing, thanking, gathering his equipment, dragging his legs and belly to the sidelines, he would find as he went the path littered with blossoms, criticisms, doubts, things that could have been done better, things to be studied, understood, practised, nurtured, and someday owned. He would see again Ando taking his *men*, see again a way he might have got ahead of Coyle, owned Yun, stymied Nygaard, see a new angle to which he might expose McCandless, Tamanaha. He would find these in his mind, and gather them—like sheet music perhaps—and bundle them in with his equipment, take them to their usual restaurant, expose them, compare them, take them home, carry them around with him, hum the tune, toy with them, rehearse them. Till next time.

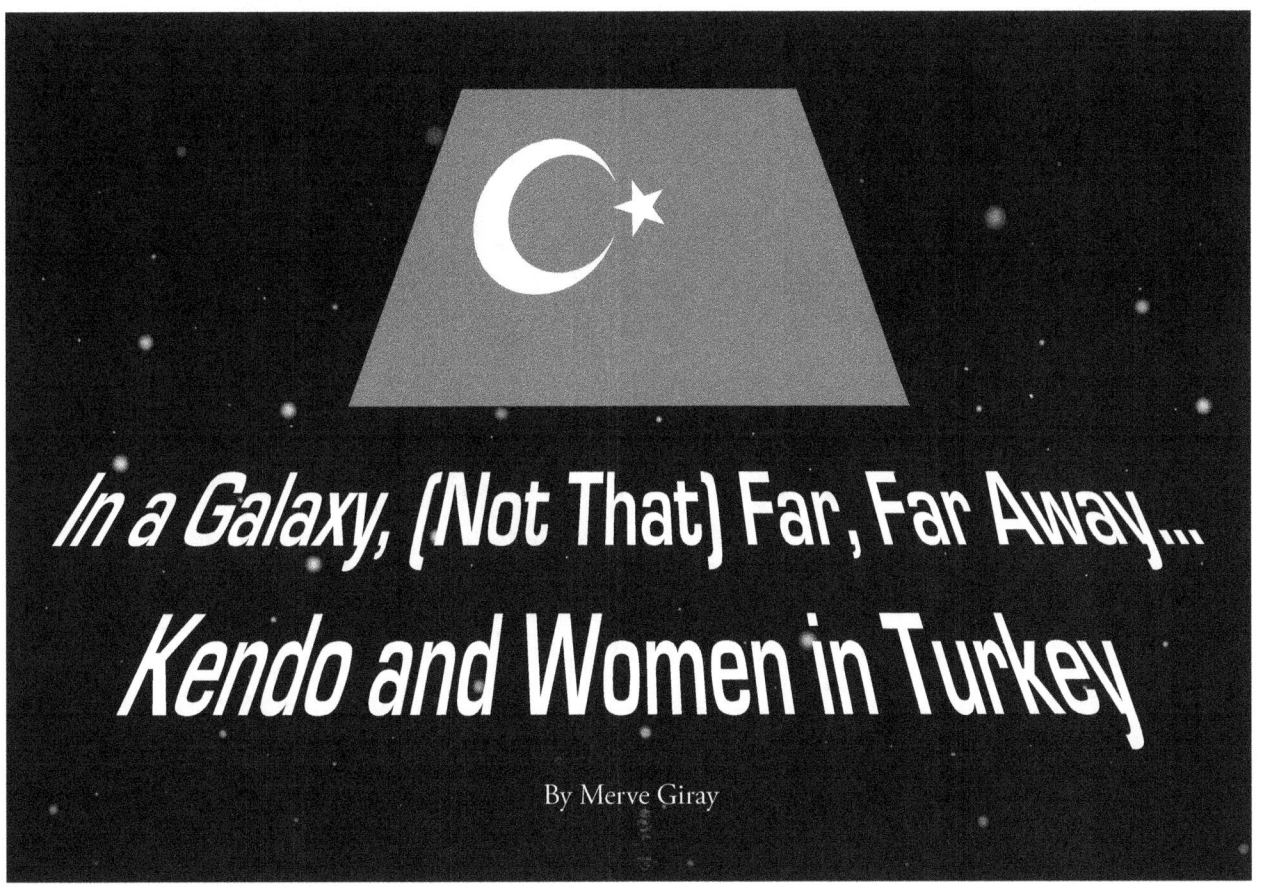

In a Galaxy, (Not That) Far, Far Away...
Kendo and Women in Turkey

By Merve Giray

I was very excited when I was asked to write this article because it was a great opportunity for me to look into how kendo has developed in Turkey, what it has become, and where women stand in the scheme of things. This report is by no means supposed to be a definitive account, but I hope it will give insight into kendo in Turkey.

A Brief History

There have been a few important events in the history of kendo in Turkey:

- The first two dojo in Turkey were founded in 1999: Istanbul Kendo Club by Egemen Doğan; Kenshikai Kendo Club by Mine Erşen.
- Training in Ankara began in 2004 through the efforts of Matsumuro-sensei and Kubo-sensei. People who practised under them then founded the Ankara Kendo and Iaido Association in 2007. Later, university dojo like ODTÜ and Bilkent opened.
- In 2008, a group from Istanbul Kendo Club founded the Boğaziçi Kendo Club, also in Istanbul. Presently, Istanbul has two dojo, and Ankara has four that train regularly and are registered with the European Kendo Federation (EKF).
- Since 2006, the Turkey Kendo Championships has been held annually, with team and individual categories.
- There have been two summer camps in Turkey so far that have brought people together from different dojo in Turkey and abroad.
- An event named "Ankara Kendo Days" is now held annually. It is a two-day seminar and it is led by different high-level European or Japanese kendoka.

Even though karate, aikido and judo are well-known and practised throughout Turkey, kendo is only found in Istanbul, Ankara and Izmir. However, the martial arts in general are not highly respected or funded in Turkey like "regular" sports such as football or tennis. This might be because of differences in the Western and Eastern understanding of the martial arts. I think Turkey can be considered Western in this regard. The martial arts are looked at as practical ways in which to defeat adversaries. The question most commonly asked of Turkish kendoka is, "If a mugger attacks you in the street when you're alone, will you be able to beat them?" If you cannot do this with your chosen martial art, what you do is considered useless, or at least not so serious.

It is difficult for people to accept that kendo goes beyond this, and is a method of communication and self-improvement. Misinterpretation is a big obstacle

to the development of kendo in Turkey. It also affects finding venues in which to train, for holding events, and obtaining funding. Furthermore, after starting kendo, it takes time to overcome the idea that kendo is not just a "sport" or "all about simply beating or hitting people". Those who accept that kendo is something much more than that, and know that it is a long, hard road, try to spread it and make it understandable to others.

Women's Situation in Turkish Kendo

Of the 84 people in Turkey who are currently registered with the EKF (meaning that they are *shodan* or above), 20 of them are women, made up of one 3-dan, eight 2-dan and 11 *shodan*. For *ikkyū* and below, the number is over 100. Some of the women also hold grades in iaido, and the only person with a dan grade in jodo in Turkey is a woman. Turkey's first international kendo award went to a woman – a fighting spirit award at the 2011 European Kendo Championships. Women also took part in founding the Turkish Kendo Association and had roles in its administration. Thus, the contribution of women to kendo and budo in Turkey has been great.

Issues with Women and Kendo

While generally speaking boys are much more physically active than girls from childhood, and are encouraged more to participate in physical activities, women tend to have much less stamina and muscular power compared to men.[1] The age at which people generally start kendo in Turkey is around 20, and because a woman's body is already developed by this age, it requires more dedication, endurance and practice if they want to keep up with the physical needs of kendo. Furthermore, gender norms assert that women should be reserved, calm and fragile, and as such, kendo may be intimidating because of the attributes like aggressiveness, dependence on muscular power and close, physical contact that kendo possesses.

"Annihilation of the feminine (…) causes alert or a sense of crisis in the world of masculine domination."[2] This is a problem for women because losing feminine characteristics, both physically and behaviourally, is not desirable in Turkey. Based on experience the actual problem here is getting women to start kendo. Once in, I have not encountered a woman who has quit

---

1 Vilhjalmsson, R and Kristjansdottir, G. "Gender Differences in Physical Activity in Older Children and Adolescents: The Central Role of Organized Sport", in *Social Science & Medicine* (Vol.56), pp.363-374, 2003.

2 Manzenreiter, W. "Physical Education and the Curriculum of Gender Reproduction. Making Body Regiémes in Japan", p.16.

2nd Kendo Camp in Turkey

kendo because of her home or child responsibilities, or because she cannot cope with kendo's physical demands.

Also, I can say that it is very easy to spot the differences in the treatment of female kendoka by male kendoka in Turkey. There is no consensus on how to treat women in the dojo, and it is not even necessary to treat them differently. While some men do not fully commit to striking *kote* or doing *tsuki* or *tai-atari* against women during *kihon* practice, others do not differentiate between the gender of the opponent. I believe that both of these attitudes are somewhat problematic.

What is Ideal?

As mentioned in the article "Developments in Japanese Women's Kendo",[3] the history of women's kendo is considerably shorter than men's. However, it is possible to see great changes being made to accommodate women in kendo. This ranges from supplying female-specific equipment that meet women's expectations, to developing different gender-specific ways to practise.

Feminists do not say that they "want to be treated like men" because they "want to be like men"; they want to be treated as equal human beings.[4] Everyone has a different level of physical capacity, muscular power, and speed.[5] Therefore, I suggest that sensei and seniors consider everyone's level of physical endurance, and push their limits accordingly. Either forcing someone way beyond their capacity, or not really pushing them at all, has unpleasant consequences and

cannot be regarded as helpful.

I had a chance to talk with Livio Lancini-sensei (R7-dan) from Italy about two different types of kendo he mentioned in his blog – "soft" and "crash".[6] Crash kendo is what we mainly see and experience: strong, rigid and largely based on muscular power. It is direct, contains close contact and considering social roles, it could be called "manly". On the other hand, soft kendo is based on timing, intuition, and flexibility. I think that this is the ideal.

Conclusion

I consider myself lucky to practise with the level of people that are in Turkey, and that I am able to take part in the seminars led by high-level kendoka from Japan and Europe. While I am only a *shodan* and relatively inexperienced, I also believe that we are at a turning point regarding teaching and practising kendo in Turkey, and also the place of Turkish women kendoka in the world. I agree with the view, "You can't be what you can't see." With the growing number of female practitioners being role models, I believe and hope that more women will get to know and want to participate in kendo.

---

3 Sylvester, K. "Developments in Japanese Women's Kendo", 2011. (Retrieved from http://www.kendoaustralia.asn.au/content/wp-ontent/uploads/2011/12/DevelopmentsinJapaneseWomenKendo.pdf, May 2013)

4 West, C. and Zimmerman, J. "Doing Gender", in *Gender & Society* (Vol.1 No.2), pp.125-151, June 1987, p.7.

5 Lorber, J. "Believing is Seeing: Biology as Ideology", in *Gender & Society* (Vol.7 No.4), pp.568-581, 1993, p.10.

6 http://donnedelkendo.blogspot.com/2006/03/noi-donne-di-livio-lancini.html

Women's Kendo in Chile

By Francesca Baradit

Kendo has been practised in Chile since 1990 when a few people started a small dojo in Santiago, the capital of the country. Since then, the number of kendo practitioners and dojo has expanded throughout the country.

The number of female kendoka has also increased. In recent years, a group of women set out to improve their kendo through basing their exercises and skills on female physical capacities. 2010 was the first year that summer training camps and *kangeiko* (intense mid-winter training) were held exclusively for women and overseen by different sensei and highly skilled female kendo practitioners. The goal of these camps was threefold:

1. To improve kendo for women
2. Create a greater unity between female kendoka
3. To continue to spread the popularity of kendo among women

Thanks to these events, in 2011 the Chilean women's kendo team achieved 1st place at the Latin-American kendo tournament in Mexico.

The result of these national female training sessions was the birth of "Kendo Domo Chile", an association of female *kenshi* in Chile. "Kendo Domo" is actually a play on words: "domo" means "women" in Mapudungun, the language of the Mapuche Indians of Chile, and it also means "thanks" in Japanese.

This year, the fourth female *gasshuku* was held in the city of Viña del Mar on May 18 and 19, 2013. It was organised by Kendo Domo Chile with the help of Dojo KaiKen in Viña del Mar and the Chilean Kendo Federation, and with sponsorship from the municipality of Viña del Mar. The seminar started on Saturday May 18 at 9:00 and ended the following day at 18:00. There were 21 participants from Chile

and Argentina, and all were highly motivated to take part in this event.

Constanza Aguilera, 3-dan and student of the International Budo University (IBU) in Japan, and Pilar Mendoza, 2-dan and captain of the Chilean women's kendo team, led the event. Under their guidance, we performed many different exercises and reviewed different techniques. We also learned new exercises based on the training regimen at the International Budo University.

First we started with lots of *ashi-sabaki* and then did *fumikomi*, *suburi*, learning how to take correct *maai*, moving backwards and forwards, and then some *kihon-waza*. In the afternoon, we started working on *oikomi* and *ōji-waza*. Sunday began with a review of the previous day before moving to *hiki-waza*. We then did *ji-geiko*, *mawari-geiko*, *kakari-geiko*, and finished the day with some matches to enhance our techniques.

The exciting part of the weekend was that so much was learned and shared by female kendoka from different parts of Chile and also Argentina. It also created a fighting spirit among all the participants which motivated them to continue learning. By the end of the event we were able to spend a pleasant time conversing about the experiences that each participant had at the seminar. We also agreed to continue practising, and to make sure that this seminar happens once a year in our country so that female practitioners from different dojo can get together to improve their skills and techniques.

薙刀団体対敵の形
The Naginata Dantai Taiteki no Kata

By Baptiste Tavernier

Introduction

In the previous issue of *Kendo World*, we introduced the *Naginatadō Kihon Dōsa*, teaching guidelines featuring a set of five generic *kata* that were published at the beginning of 1941 by the Dai Nippon Butokukai in order to promote a unified form of naginata in schools. We saw that this initiative somehow failed because of the antagonism between the two major naginata *ryūha*: the Jikishin Kage-ryū and the Tendō-ryū. Exponents of the Tendō-ryū tradition considered the *Naginatadō Kihon Dōsa* to be a simplification of the Jikishin Kage-ryū style rather than a unification of different traditions, and thus refused to follow the new guidelines. As a result, the intended unification of naginata did not occur, and the situation in schools remained unchanged: children instructed by a Jikishin Kage-ryū instructor learned the Butokukai's *Naginatadō Kihon Dōsa*, while classes with a Tendō-ryū instructor endeavored to practise the *kata* of that tradition. Schools where naginata classes were instructed by teachers from neither the Jikishin Kage-ryū nor the Tendō-ryū, sometimes the Butokukai's guidelines were adopted, and sometimes rejected in favour of such as teaching materials as *kata* or techniques from other traditions, such as the Katori Shintō-ryū.

The Nihon Kokumin Naginatadō Kyōhon

In this rather confused state of affairs, an almost unknown but noteworthy initiative was that of Niino Kyūhei. He decided to ignore the Butokukai's new guidelines and did not affiliate with an existing naginata *ryūha*, but rather devised his own methodology. He created exercises that would impart basic naginata moves and advanced techniques in order to develop in his students practical skills for *shiai*. He also conbined those different techniques into a new set of five *kata* entitled the Naginata Dantai Taiteki no Kata. He published *Nihon Kokumin Naginatadō Kyōhon* (The Japanese People's Naginatadō Textbook) in November 1941, which served as naginata teaching material at the Ootsu Women's High School in Shiga prefecture.

This book was in a way revolutionary. The Butokukai's *Naginatadō Kihon Dōsa* did not constitute a modern system where a *naginata* would face another *naginata*, but promoted instead the old pattern of a *naginata* facing a sword, which is inconvenient as a school teaching material because the children had to become proficient in the use of two very different weapons in a short period of time. Certainly aware of this issue, Niino Kyūhei devised instead a *naginata* versus *naginata* method.

Dedication and foreword

The book starts with a dedication by Miwa Kikusaburō, Principal of Ootsu Women's High School in Shiga prefecture:

> Niino Kyūhei-sensei, *naginata-jutsu* Renshi and kendo R5-dan from the Dai Nippon Butokukai, is a long-known budo scholar. He recently wrote a textbook about kendo and contributed much to the pedagogy of this art. He also supports innovative opinions regarding *naginata* teaching methodologies. Niino Kyūhei-sensei remains sceptical regarding the sole repetition of old naginata forms or "*kata*", and rather advocates that the students learn basic moves and continue further with *shiai*. He believes that the students' interest in naginata will grow as they engage in mock fights, and that they should ultimately experience the quintessence of both spirit and technique.
> Indeed, such farsightedness deserves our respect.
> In order to discipline minds and bodies at our school, we decided to make *naginatadō* mandatory for our senior students. We are proud of the great results we obtained and will always be grateful to Niino Kyūhei-sensei's enthusiastic and forceful guidance. We should be delighted that *naginatadō* is now a compulsory subject in both elementary schools and high schools. The spirit of budo will spread, now that the youth have the opportunity to study all its techniques.
> However, for that to become a reality, the lack of suitable teaching manuals was, until now, extremely regrettable. This is why our qualified sensei, after many years of research, wrote this book, the *Nihon Kokumin Naginatadō Kyōhon*. This textbook is easy

to read and the main points are easy to grasp.
To conclude, I believe that this book will contribute in many ways to the disciplining of minds and bodies, and will meet the expectations of this craving world. This autumn, the whole country will be brewing with the exaltations of budo spirit and body-forging.
I sincerely recommend this book.

      Miwa Kikusaburō, August 1941

The dedication is followed by Niino Kyūhei's words of introduction. In this, the author outlines the spirit of bushido and the ideal of *yamato-damashi* (Japanese soul), and introduces some aspects of naginata history. He explains his motivation for publishing his book in the last part of the introduction:

> Recently, budo's prosperity suddenly reached the extremes. *Naginata-jutsu* finally gets the opportunity to rise as a budo for girls and to spread as a very pertinent way to foster virtue in women, to nurture the spirit, and to discipline the mind and body. This is especially true since naginata is instructed in girl's schools. I also rejoice over the fact that naginata is now taught in elementary schools as well.
>
> However, each *ryūha* has its own different and complicated style, its weapons and their peculiar usages. Some traditions also have some quite irrational ways of using the body. All this, from a pedagogical point of view, can become a great obstacle. As I mentioned earlier, modern *naginatadō* is a method created in order to discipline and nurture the mind and the body. It is not necessary anymore to instruct in schools the difficult *kata* of different old traditions. I believe that what is most important is to teach the spirit of *naginatadō*, along with a practical way of using the techniques.
>
> Nowadays, as we live under the Kokka Shintaisei (national politic), it is imperative to devise a suitable naginata methodology expurgated of the aforementioned obstacles.
>
> For about ten years, I studied *naginata-jutsu*. As I humbly wished to contribute to the development of naginata, I decided to introduce to the naginata instructors in girl's schools, elementary schools and high schools, this very simple and practical method based upon the fruit of my research.
>
> With regards to what is published in this book, the pedagogy is based on group-instruction for beginners, made of simple representative basic moves and the five series of the Dantai Taiteki no Kata. I believe this is an extremely adequate teaching material for schools. I do realise that due to my lack of competence and my poor writing, it cannot be faultless, but it is my hope that various wise instructors will perfect this method with their experience and research.
>
>   July 1941, The author

The militaristic flavor of Niino's method

Niino's method was released one month before Japan entered the Pacific War. In 1941, a significant change was made in schools when "physical education" was officially renamed "physical discipline". The militarisation of education in Japan was by then almost reaching its climax, and it is thus not surprising to find many militaristic elements in Niino's pedagogy. "Discipline" being a keyword of the time, the guidelines naturally start by stressing its importance in a short paragraph entitled "The Meaning of Discipline":

> "Budo", our National Spirit, is not about the mere practice of techniques, but is a way to discipline our mind and body, nurture our potential power, and at the same time remind us of the teachings of the five ethics: *jin* (benevolence), *gi* (justice), *rei* (courtesy), *chi* (wisdom) and *shin* (sincerity). With the spirit of bushido as a base, he who studies budo will grow his mind and body stronger and stronger, will accomplish his duty, will endure every hardship, and by conjugating the two ways of literacy and military, will become a splendid person who contributes to his nation.

This is followed by the "Four Instructions on Discipline"

> * **One who studies budo shall always demonstrate correct manners.**
> * **The dojo is a place where one polishes mind and body. One shall always keep the dojo clean and shall devotedly discipline mind and body with a solemn attitude.**
> * **One shall always keep training gear and garments clean.**
> * **One shall handle with great care *bōgu*, *tachi* or *naginata*, as if they were one's soul.**

The above instructions on discipline concern budo in general. When it comes to budo for women, it is particularly crucial that the students show demeanour and etiquette with grace, and display the feminine virtues of old Japan.

The militarisation of the training routine described in the textbook is clear. For example, one will notice that every single move is made under commands given by the instructor. The class begins with:

"Migi he narae!—Naore!"
(line up, face to the right!—At ease!);

Uchikomi kiri-gaeshi in formation

"*Zenretsu nanpō mae he!—Gūsū nanpō mae he!*" (Front row step forward!—Even numbers step forward!);
"*Keirei!—Naore!*";
"*Saikeirei!—Naore!*";
"*Orishiki!—Rei!—Kiritsu!*"
(the bowing sequence)

The instructor also gives commands for every posture, strike, and block, and even every move featured in the *kata*.

Niino also introduced the idea of training in formation, like a military unit. Girls had to go through a routine called *uchikomi kiri-gaeshi*, arranged in a quincunx in several rows. The term *uchi* (strike) that was used before in naginata training was also replaced by *zangeki* (slash). *Uchikomi kiri-gaeshi* consists of nine techniques performed one after the other, left and right:

- *Shomen* cut from *jōdan* (left and right)
- *Men* cut from *hassō* (left and right)
- *Sune* cut from *hassō* (left and right)
- *Dō* cut from *waki* (left and right)
- *kote* cut from *waki* (left and right)
- *Tsuki* with the *ishizuki* to the chest from *waki* (left)
- *Kote-shomen* cuts from *hassō* (left)
- *Tsuki* to the chest from *chūdan* (right)
- *Tsuki* to the throat from *gedan* (right)
- *Tsuki* with the *ishizuki* to the chest from *waki* (right)
- *Kote-shomen* cuts from *hassō* (right)
- *Tsuki* to the chest from *chūdan* (left)
- *Tsuki* to the throat from *gedan* (left)

Finally, Niino introduces the five *kata* of the Naginata Dantai Taiteki no Kata, which can be translated as "Naginata Kata in Formation Against the Enemy". Each series features very easy, but in fact very practical techniques, which have to be performed in formation as well. Pictures in the original textbook show three pairs of girls moving at the same pace, like a unit.

In *ippon-me*, *shikata* dodges a thrust made in the *jūken-jutsu* style (bayonet technique) and ripostes with a *sune* cut. The next series is based on the same pattern, *shikata* dodges a thrust made to the throat, but strikes back with a *men* cut. In *sanbon-me*, *shikata* blocks a direct *sune* cut, then evades to the side and ripostes with a *men* cut. *Yonhon-me* is the opposite of the previous series, with a *men* block followed by a *sune* cut. Finally, in *gohon-me*, *shikata* dodges a very big *men* cut from *jōdan* and and ripostes with a mowing *dō* cut.

Reception

It is hard to ascertain the impact that *Nihon Kokumin Naginatadō Kyōhon* had on the naginata world during the war. This method focused on *naginata* versus *naginata* training and was made of basic strikes that could be used in *shiai* and easily conbined in *kata*. Although it was clearly a long-awaited evolution in term of pedagogy, it seems that its influence did not get past the scope of Shiga prefecture. Niino Kyūhei's textbook is still unknown to most naginata practitioners and instructors in Japan and around the world. Nevertheless, it is worth studying, as it stands as a precursor of Sakakida Yaeko's research that would later be instrumental in the establishment of modern naginata, based on the Shikake-ōji and *shiai*. Interestingly (although it is not possible to tell for sure if Sakakida's work was influenced by Niino Kyūhei), series 1, 3, 4 & 5 of the Naginata Dantai Taiteki no Kata look familiar, as one can find some of their technical elements in the Shikake-ōji and the *kata* that are currently taught in naginata.

The following is a translation of the Naginata Dantai Taiteki no Kata guidelines as they appear in the *Nihon Kokumin Naginatadō Kyōhon*.

Naginata Dantai Taiteki no Kata
(Naginata Kata in Formation Against the Enemy)

The *kata* starts with a standing bow.

First, *uchidachi* and *shidachi* face the *shōmen* (or the *kamiza*) holding their *naginata* and bow. They then bow to each other, draw near and perform *orishiki* (the *kissaki* are slightly crossed) and a *sonkyo-rei*. Finally, they stand up while assuming *udemaki* and from the left foot take three steps backward.

The yells must be natural and shouted during the strikes, with *kiai*.

The *kata* ends like it starts, but in reverse order.

First, perform *orishiki* and a *sonkyo-rei*. From the left foot take three steps backward and bow to each other. Finally, *uchidachi* and *shidachi* face the *shōmen* (or the *kamiza*) and bow. That concludes the Kata Against the Enemy.

Follow the commands from beginning to end when performing the Dantai Taiteki no Kata.

Note: When training with one partner only instead of a formation, move according to each other's *ki*.

Kata opening

Face the shōmen (kamiza)

Assume udemaki

Bow to the shōmen (kamiza)

Bow to each other

Orishiki

Sonkyo-rei

Stand up while assuming udemaki

Step backward

Dai ippon-me

Command: *"Ippon-me yōi!"*
Outline: **Uchidachi** *and* **shidachi** *both assume* omote chūdan-no-kamae.

Command: *"Dōsa hajime!"*
Outline: *Uchidachi* and *shidachi* **take two steps from the right foot and come in contact at the** *maai*.

Command: *"Tsuke!"*
Outline: *Uchidachi* **takes one step forward from the left foot and thrusts to** *shidachi*'s **chest.** *Shidachi* **absorbs** *uchidachi*'s **thrust (***nayasu***) by avoiding the** *kissaki*, **and strikes** *sune*.

Command: *"Zanshin!"*
Outline: *Uchidachi* **and** *shidachi* **demonstrate** *zanshin* **while going back to** *omote chūdan-no-kamae*.

Command: *"Ato he!"*
Outline: *Uchidachi* **and** *shidachi* **return in** *udemaki* **and from the left foot take three steps backward.**

Assume omote chūdan-no-kamae

Enter into the maai. Uchidachi is about to thrust

Uchidachi thrusts to the chest; shidachi strikes sune

Go back to omote chūdan-no-kamae, and demonstrate zanshin

Dai nihon-me

Command: *"Nihon-me yōi!"*
Outline: *Uchidachi* **assumes** *omote gedan* **and** *shidachi* **assumes** *omote chūdan*.

Command: *"Dōsa hajime!"*
Outline: *Uchidachi* **and** *shidachi* **take two steps from the right foot and come in contact at the** *maai*.

Command: *"Tsuke!"*
Outline: *Uchidachi* **takes one step forward from the left foot and thrusts to** *shidachi*'s **throat.** *Shidachi* **performs a** *suri-age* **onto** *uchidachi*'s *kissaki*, **moves slightly diagonally to the left and strikes** *men*.

Command: *"Zanshin!"*
Outline: *Uchidachi* **and** *shidachi* **demonstrate** *zanshin* **while going back to** *omote chūdan no kamae*.
Command: *"Ato he!"*
Outline: *Uchidachi* **and** *shidachi* **return in** *udemaki* **and from the left foot take three steps backward.**

Uchidachi assumes gedan and shidachi chūdan

Enter into the maai. Uchidachi is about to thrust

Uchidachi thrusts to the throat. Shidachi strikes men

Go back to omote chūdan-no-kamae, and demonstrate zanshin

Dai sanbon-me

Command: "*Sanbon-me yōi!*"
Outline: *Uchidachi* **assumes** *omote wakigamae* **and** *shidachi* **assumes** *omote chūdan*.

Command: "*Dōsa hajime!*"
Outline: *Uchidachi* and *shidachi* **take two steps from the right foot and come in contact at the** *maai*.
Command: "*Utte!*"
Outline: *Uchidachi* **steps forward with the right foot and strikes** *shidachi*'s *sune*. *Shidachi* **steps back with the left foot while performing a** *suri-sage* **onto** *uchidachi*'s *naginata*, **then an** *ukenagashi* **with the** *ishizuki*. *Shidachi* **moves from the left foot diagonally to the left and strikes** *uchidachi*'s *men*.

Command: "*Zanshin!*"
Outline: *Uchidachi* **goes back to** *ura chūdan-no-kamae* **and** *shidachi* **to** *omote chūdan-no-kamae*. **Both demonstrate** *zanshin*.

Command: "*Ato he!*"
Outline: *Uchidachi* **and** *shidachi* **return in** *udemaki* **and from the left foot take three steps backward.**

Uchidachi assumes wakigamae and shidachi chūdan

Enter into the maai. Uchidachi is about to strike

Uchidachi strikes sune. Shidachi performs ukenagashi

Shidachi strikes men

Uchidachi goes back to ura chūdan and shidachi to omote chūdan. Zanshin

Dai yonhon-me

Command: "*Yonhon-me yōi!*"
Outline: *Uchidachi* **assumes** *omote hassō* **and** *shidachi* **assumes** *omote chūdan*.

Command: "*Dōsa hajime!*"
Outline: *Uchidachi* and *shidachi* **take two steps from the right foot and come in contact at the** *maai*.

Command: "*Utte!*"
Outline: *Uchidachi* **steps forward with the right foot and strikes** *shidachi*'s *naname men*. *Shidachi*

steps back with the left foot while performing an *ukenagashi* (*shidachi*'s *kissaki* goes downward to the back while the *ishizuki* goes upward). *Shidachi* moves from the left foot diagonally to the left and strikes *uchidachi*'s *sune*.

Command: "*Zanshin!*"
Outline: *Uchidachi* goes back to *ura chūdan-no-kamae* and *shidachi* to *omote chūdan-no-kamae*. Both demonstrate *zanshin*.

Command: "*Ato he!*"
Outline: *Uchidachi* and *shidachi* return in *udemaki* and from the left foot take three steps backward.

Uchidachi assumes hassō and shidachi chūdan

Enter into the maai. Uchidachi is about to strike

Uchidachi strikes men. Shidachi performs ukenagashi

Shidachi strikes sune

Uchidachi goes back to ura chūdan and shidachi to omote chūdan. Zanshin

Dai gohon-me

Command: "*Gohon-me yōi!*"
Outline: *Uchidachi* assumes *omote jōdan* and *shidachi* assumes *omote chūdan*.

Command: "*Dōsa hajime!*"
Outline: *Uchidachi* and *shidachi* take two steps from the right foot and come in contact at the *maai*.

Command: "*Utte!*"
Outline: *Uchidachi* steps forward with the right foot and strikes *shidachi*'s *shōmen*. *Shidachi* steps back with the left foot while performing an *ukenagashi* (*shidachi*'s *kissaki* goes downward to the back while the *ishizuki* goes upward). *Shidachi* moves from the left foot diagonally to the left and strikes *uchidachi*'s *dō*.

Command: "*Zanshin!*"
Outline: *Uchidachi* goes back to *ura chūdan-no-kamae* and *shidachi* to *omote chūdan-no-kamae*. Both demonstrate *zanshin*.

Command: "*Ato he!*"
Outline: *Uchidachi* and *shidachi* return in *udemaki* and from the left foot take three steps backward.

Uchidachi assumes jōdan and shidachi chūdan

Enter into the maai. Uchidachi is about to strike

Uchidachi strikes men. Shidachi performs ukenagashi

Shidachi strikes dō

Uchidachi goes back to ura chūdan and shidachi to omote chūdan. Zanshin

Kata closing

Orishiki

Sonkyo-rei

Take three steps back

Bow

Face the shōmen (kamiza)

Bow

The kata is over

Bujutsu Jargon Part 4

Bruce Flanagan MA (Lecturer - Nanzan University)

Reference guide covering various bujutsu-related terminology

\# 25 稽古 *keiko*

An old word for 'training' or 'practice' still frequently used today. The first character *kei / kangaeru* means 'to consider' or 'to research' and the second character *inishie* means 'things of the past' or 'ancient times'. Often written in *hiragana*, this verbal-noun refers to practice or rehearsal in performing arts such as music, theatre, flower arrangement, tea ceremony and disciplines such as the martial arts. In contrast with a term such as *renshū* (training), *keiko* includes a nuance of cultivation or spiritual refinement.

Hierarchical class system of the Edo Period instated by the Tokugawa shogunate which divided the mainstream population into four tiers. Samurai (*shi*) maintained primary status, followed by farmers (*nō*), artisans and craftsmen (*kō*), and merchants (*shō*). Collectively the four classes were referred to as *shimin* (四民). Those whose lot in life relegated them to performing work considered undesirable by the four main classes were often ostracized to the lowly status of 'inhuman' outcastes (*hinin* or *eta*).

\# 26 士農工商 *shi-nō-kō-shō*

\# 27 大日本武徳会 Dai-Nihon Butokukai

The Dai-Nihon Butoku-kai (Greater-Japan Martial Virtue Society) was formed in 1895 to promote the practice of martial arts. Its original *honbu* headquarters were situated in the grounds of Heian Jingu Shrine in Kyoto where the Budo Center is now located, and *shibu* branches called Butokuden (Hall of Martial Virtue) were located in each prefecture. The organisation was ordered to disband after WWII but reformed shortly thereafter on a much smaller scale. It is now registered as a general corporation and continues to promote and preserve martial arts through practice and demonstrations. Overseas branches now exist in many countries.

Old word meaning a 'competition'. The first character *shi* means 'to test' and the second character *ai* means 'to meet', referring to 'testing skills against an opponent', although the word was also written 仕合 with the same pronunciation. Still used today in martial arts and sports, the term may widely mean a tennis 'game', a boxing 'match', a boat 'race', or even a surfing 'contest'. Meaning may extend to a 'tournament' or 'championship' but events of a large enough scale are usually called *taikai*. Types of *shiai* may include mixed style tournaments (*taryū-jiai* 他流試合), contests between different martial arts or sports (*ishu-jiai* 異種試合), and goodwill matches (*shinzen-jiai* 親善試合).

\# 28 試合 *shiai*

#29 鎖鎌 kusari-gama

A chain (*kusari*) and sickle (*kama*) weapon believed to have been devised around the beginning of the Edo Period. The basic version consists of a metal blade attached perpendicularly to a wooden handle which is fitted with a long chain weighted with a metal head (*fundō*) at its end. It can be used at close or medium-range and serves as a one-handed cutting, flailing and ensnaring weapon. The wielder generally attempts to entangle the enemy's body or weapon with the end of the chain while outside of the enemy's attacking range and then disarms the enemy at a safe distance or engages at close quarters with the sickle. Use of the *kusari-gama* is one of the 18 skills of the *bugei-jūhappan* and is still practised in a number of *koryū* schools.

#30 鞘当て saya-ate

Saya is the 'scabbard' of a sword and *ate* is 'a collision'. A *saya-ate* or 'scabbard-collision' (also *saya-togame*) occurs when two individuals pass each other closely enough that the ends of their sword scabbards crash together. *Saya-ate* were often the cause of arguments, fights and duels and, consequently, these altercations themselves also came to be known as *saya-ate*. The term is now used to refer to an argument or fight that occurs over petty pride or to describe two men fighting over a woman.

#31 武術 bujutsu

The Chinese word *wushu* has long been a part of the Japanese vernacular; it is pronounced *bujutsu* and means 'combat techniques'. Although the term is ambiguous and varied in meaning, Japanese *bujutsu* generally constituted 'techniques' designed for killing an opponent, in contrast to *budō*, or modern martial 'ways/arts', which now focus on self-defence and self-improvement. In Japan's feudal past, warfare and military strategy was called *heihō* or *hyōhō* (ways of war) and the exponent was called a *heihō-ka* or *hyōhō-ka*. During the Edo period, when training for battle became highly structured and stylised, martial arts were referred to as *bujutsu* or *bugei* and practitioners were called *bujutsu-ka* or *bugei-sha*. The Meiji period saw great leaps forward in the modernisation of *bujutsu* arts and Kanō Jigorō was the first to use the character 道 (*dō* - way/art) when he created *jūdō* from various styles of *jūjutsu*. This trend proved popular and, among others, *kendō* was developed from *kenjutsu/gekken*, *kyūdō* from *kyūjutsu*, and *iaidō* from *iaijutsu*. The term *budō-ka* replaced the term *bujutsu-ka* with the connotation being that the *budō-ka* strive to cultivate themselves through the practice of martial arts rather than simply learning how to defeat an opponent and, as such, a strong delineation was drawn between feudal combat techniques (*kinsei-bujutsu*) and modern martial ways/arts (*gendai-budō*).

Bibliography

- *Budō no Kotoba - Gendai ni Ikasu Shōbu no Tessoku*, PHP Kenkyūsho (ed.), 1987.
- *Bujutsu Jiten (Zusetsu)*, Osano J., Shinkigensha, 2003.
- *Kendō Wa-Ei Jiten*, Zen Nihon Kendō Renmei (ed.), Satō Inshokan Inc., 2000.
- *Kōjien (Daigohan)*, Iwanami Shoten, 2004.
- *Nichijōgo no naka no Budō Kotoba Gogen Jiten*, Katō H. & Nishimura R. (ed.), Tōkyōdō Shuppan, 1995.
- *Nihon Budō Jiten (Zusetsu)*, Sasama Y., Kashiwa-Shobō, 2003.
- *Sengoku Jidai Yōgo Jiten*, Togawa J., Gakushū Kenkyūsha, 2006.

Martial Aids
The "Tare Belt"

USD$65 (shipping included)

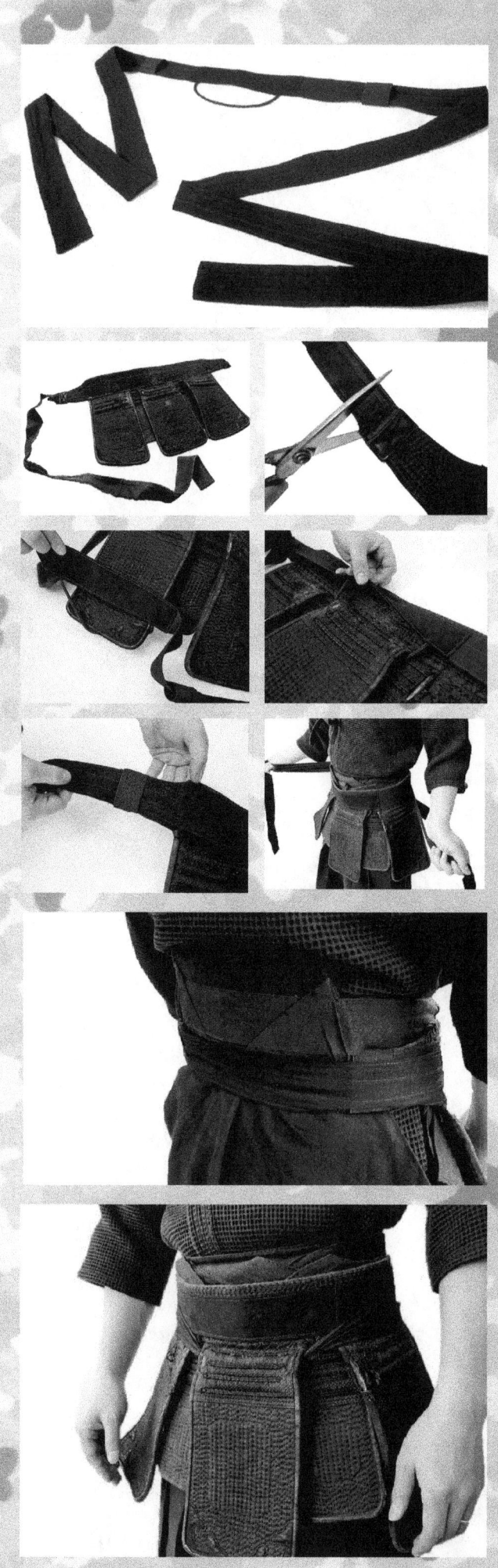

An innovative yet remarkably simple invention to reintroduce the 'Martial Aids' column, this issue of KW is reviewing the 'Tare Belt' by Shogun Kendogu.

Despite its important functions of suppressing the beer belly, holding up the trousers, and the obvious protective qualities, the *tare* and its *himo* remain a cloth and leather arrangement held together with only a few stitches. Thus, the exposure of the *tare-himo* on the side of the body render it the piece of armour that is often the first to show signs of wear. While every other piece of kendo gear is fastened with cords that are simple to replace, this is not the case when it comes to a *tare* repair job. *Tare* are costly to fix and/or replace, and then there's the shipping...

Targeted at clubs and dojo that lack the surplus cash-flow to source replacements or repairs, the staff at Shogun Kendogu are pitching the "Tare Belt" as a "cost effective way to maximise the life of the tired *tare*."

As the pictures show, it is no more than an *obi* with a few flash extras, and a couple of rubber bands for good measure. Yet, despite its underwhelming first impression, it seems to have the ability to do exactly what they say it will—provide a cheap alternative to sending an old *tare* away for repair, or buying a new one altogether.

KW's trial run of this product found that it acts just as well, if not slightly better than an *obi*, by giving the wearer more ability to tighten the *tare* around the lower abdomen – minus the potential cumbersomeness of the *obi* and *tare* combo. In this regard it is not limited to old sets of club or beginner gear. However, no one is suggesting that you should lop the *himo* off your current *tare* prematurely!

You'll also notice from the accompanying photos that the Tare Belt is barely discernible once attached.

The Tare Belt by Shogun Kendogu is made in Japan to order. Using #4,000 grade *aizome* dyed fabric, it is strong enough and light enough to be a worthwhile consideration for those who fear that tearing sound when tying up their current, worn out belly-holder-inner.

One point to consider regarding the price, shipping is included and bulk orders seem to be discounted, so it may be worthwhile considering a group order.

Go to www.shogunkendogu.com to find out more.

KENDO: A COMPREHENSIVE GUIDE TO JAPANESE SWORDSMANSHIP

By Geoff Salmon

Review by Alex Bennett

The front cover of the latest book in English on kendo shows the author in *chūdan* facing off against his opponent. A close look at his *tare* shows that his name written in *katakana* as "SARUMAN". I have known Geoff Salmon-sensei for a number of years now, but it never occurred to me that in Japanese, he is the White Wizard antagonist in J.R.R. Tolkien's fantasy novel, *The Lord of the Rings*. Ironically also, SARUMAN apparently means "man of skill". In some ways, this all seems strangely appropriate, if not a little intimidating.

Anybody who is interested in kendo surely knows Salmon. A quick search on the net for information about kendo and you are sure to encounter some of his writings. He is truly prolific, and more than qualified to write a book on kendo put out by Tuttle – the granddaddy of publishers specialising in things Japanese.

There are a few books out in English now that pretty much cover the same content in one form or another, so I was curious to see how Salmon would render his years of experience into book form. The result is an easily accessible, logically structured, well-illustrated guide for beginner to intermediate level *kenshi*. He covers all the important topics in kendo including the basic concepts, footwork, equipment, relatively detailed explanations of all the main *waza*, as well as useful sections on training methods and structuring a kendo lesson. There is also a glossary at the back, and interspersed throughout the sections are constructive explanations of various concepts such as "*Seme*, *Tame* and the Four Sicknesses", or other tenets of useful information.

The main characteristic of the content is the user-friendly explanations. Even for usually complicated terms and concepts, Salmon's descriptions are not verbose, and get straight to the point. Furthermore, all of the techniques and technical explanations are supplemented with wonderful illustrations by kendo 5-dan, Katsuya Masagaki. The illustrations are concise, and demonstrate the intricate movements of the body, hands and *shinai* from various angles with a clarity that would be difficult to depict with photographs.

Indeed, the content is across-the-board and masterfully laid out. If I were to make one criticism though, I think a short section outlining the history of kendo would not be amiss, and would have added to its comprehensiveness. Nevertheless, this is only a minor gripe, and the book will surely become a standard text for kendo aficionados of all levels. It will serve as a useful introductory text for people starting out, and a convenient reference for intermediate or even advanced practitioners. I suspect it will be of particular value to the hordes of 3 or 4-dan level *kenshi* around the world who reluctantly find themselves in instructional positions – no small responsibility. To them, I imagine this book will become a very close friend.

On that note, I would like to congratulate Geoff Salmon-sensei for his wonderful contribution to the kendo world, and recommend that all kendo enthusiasts purchase the book, but keep it in your *bōgu* bag rather than on your bookshelf. It was written to be used.

Tuttle Publishing; Original edition (May 7, 2013)
192 pages, English, Paperback $11.32, Kindle $9.45

ADVERTISEMENT

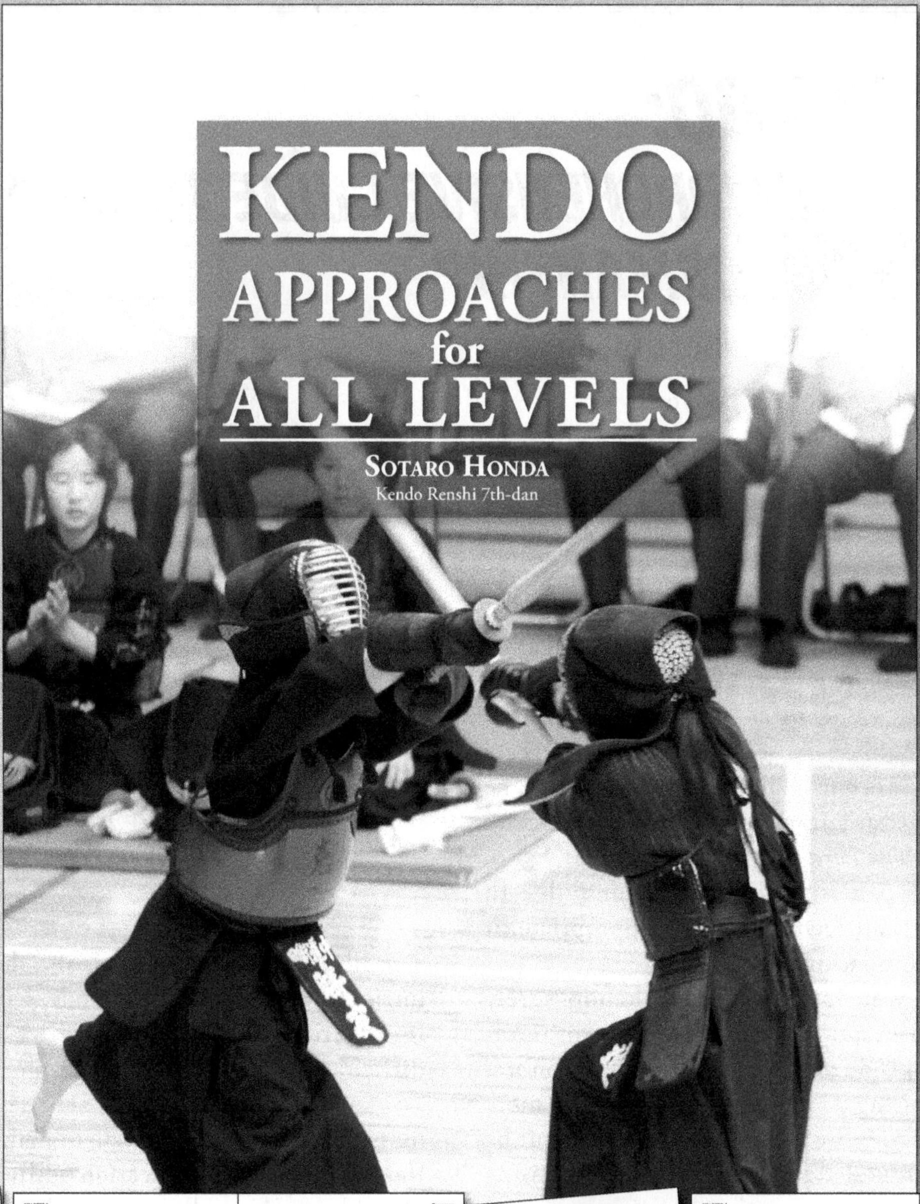

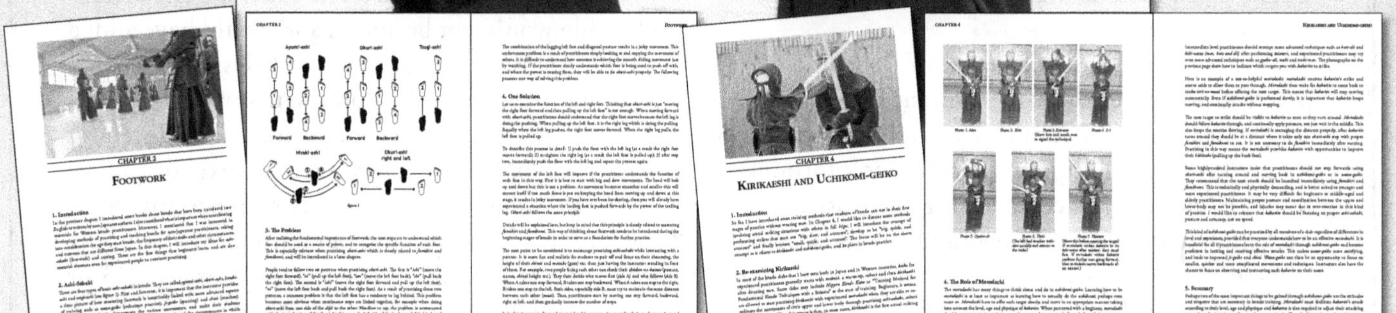

Kendo World is proud to announce our latest publication to enhance your understanding of kendo. Dr. Sotaro Honda (R7-dan), student of H8-dan Masatake Sumi-sensei, has been a longtime contributor to Kendo World, and has spent much of his kendo career helping international kenshi. His latest book is a must have for all practitioners and instructors, and explains various aspects of kendo training in a way that is both accessible and eye-opening. He covers the basics from footwork, to various *keiko* methods such as kakari-geiko and *ji-geiko*, and offers many useful hints for *shiai* strategy. Buy this book on Kindle as a download, or as a hard copy. See **www.kendo-world.com** for more details!

KENDO —Approaches For All Levels—

Sotaro Honda Kendo Renshi 7-dan   B5 size 102 pages B/W **$25.00**

To order, visit **www.kendo-world.com** more information, mail to **info@kendo-world.com**

Published by **BUNKASHA** INTERNATIONAL CORPORATION / 2498-8 Oyumi-chō, Chūōku, Chiba-shi, Chiba, JAPAN 260-0813

www.ingramcontent.com/pod-product-compliance
Lightning Source LLC
Chambersburg PA
CBHW080856090426
42735CB00014B/3168